The History of a Myth

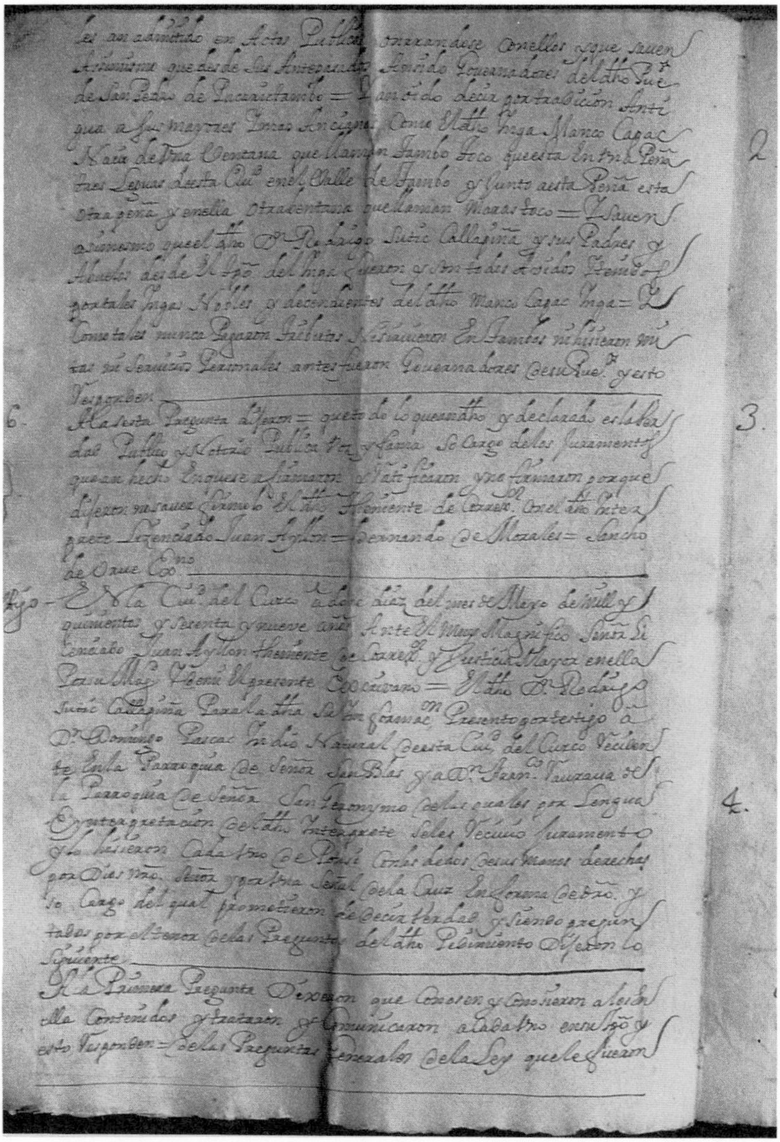

A page from the Callapiña Document (Appendix, folio 3v)

GARY URTON

THE HISTORY OF A MYTH

*Pacariqtambo and the
Origin of the Inkas*

 UNIVERSITY OF TEXAS PRESS, AUSTIN

First Edition, 1990

Requests for permission to reproduce material from
this work should be sent to Permissions, University
of Texas Press, Box 7819, Austin, Texas
78713-7819.

⊚ The paper used in this publication meets the
minimum requirements of American National
Standard for Information Sciences—Permanence of
Paper for Printed Library Materials, ANSI
Z39.48-1984.

Library of Congress Cataloging-in-Publication Data
Urton, Gary, 1946–
    The history of a myth : Pacariqtambo and the
origin of the Inkas / by Gary Urton.—1st ed.
        p.   cm.
    Includes bibliographical references.
    ISBN 0-292-73051-9 (alk. paper).—ISBN
0-292-73057-8 (pbk : alk. paper)
    1. Incas—History.   2. Incas—Religion and
mythology.   3. Indians of South America—Peru—
Paccarictambo—Religion and mythology.
4. Paccarictambo (Peru)—History.   I. Title.
F3429.U88   1990
985'.01—dc20   89-25074
                                          CIP

For Mark and Jason

Contents

Illustrations

Plates

Acknowledgments

Many people have generously provided me with help, advice, and support during both the fieldwork and the writing-up stages of work on this book. I would first like to thank my wife, Julia L. Meyerson, who was my companion throughout most of the two and one-half years that I carried out fieldwork in Pacariqtambo (see Meyerson, 1990). Julia helped transcribe several of the documents that were used in the preparation of this study and she drew the figures. Without her keen observations and good advice and companionship in the field, this study would not have been possible. I would especially like to acknowledge her support during the time when she, our son, Jason, and I were all laid up with hepatitis in Cuzco (from November 1987 through January 1988); it was during this respite from field-work that I was able to complete the first draft of the manuscript.

Jean-Jacques Decoster, a graduate student in anthropology at Cor-nell University, served as my field assistant in Pacariqtambo in 1987. Jean-Jacques provided invaluable assistance and advice, as well as a keen and critical perspective on the ethnographic details of the organization of settlements in the district of Pacariqtambo. Most of what I know about the villages of P'irca and Warubamba derives from the fieldwork that Jean-Jacques carried out in those communities.

For his great good humor, unflagging friendship, and countless hours of patient instruction on the organization and history of Paca-riqtambo, I thank my friend don Baltazar Quispe Herrera. Baltazar, his wife, Teresa, and the other members of their family offered Julia and me constant friendship and support during our fieldwork in the village.

I am extremely grateful to the following people for reading and commenting on earlier drafts of this manuscript: Brian Bauer, Jean-Jacques Decoster, John Hyslop, Julia Meyerson, Deborah Poole, Robert Randall, Joanne Rappaport, Johan Reinhard, Frank Salomon, Michael Thomas, and Tom Zuidema. I thank John Murra for his kind words of encouragement on the occasion of my primordial attempt to articulate the ideas that evolved into this monograph (at the Northeast Regional Meetings on Andean Archaeology and Ethnohistory, Amherst, Massachusetts, 1983). I absolve all of these individuals of any responsibility for the opinions expressed, and errors that remain, in this study. I would also like to express my appreciation to Eulogio Coronel González and Brian Bauer for their help in obtaining copies of documents in the Coronel collection.

Support for the ethnographic and archival research on which this study is based was provided in 1981–1982 by a postdoctoral research grant from the National Science Foundation (#BNS-8106254); in the summer of 1984 by the Research Council at Colgate University; in 1985 and 1987 by the John Ben Snow Memorial Trust (Syracuse, New York); and in 1987–1988 by a sabbatical leave and a Picker Research Fellowship from Colgate University. I acknowledge with sincere thanks the support provided by these organizations and institutions.

The History of a Myth

1. The Mythic Dimensions of Inka History

Introduction

One very common theme in the origin myths of ancient kingdoms and states around the world is the depiction of the founder-ancestors as "strangers," or outsiders, who appear seemingly from nowhere—or perhaps from some specified place in the distance—and who undergo a period of primordial wandering before arriving at their homeland. The ancestors, often represented as characters possessing supernatural qualities or advanced technologies, wander from place to place, like exiles in the land that they are destined to rule. The period of wandering finally comes to an end when the ancestors arrive at a place—a mythic re-echoing of geography familiar to the narrator—at which they establish their capital. From this place and time begins the local tradition of mythic history, filled variously with episodes of conquests, skillful manipulation of alliances, and other such stratagems through which the kingdom or state slowly begins to emerge in the form known to the living generation of descendants (Hocart, 1970 [1936]; Sahlins, 1985).

Such, in schematic form, is the basic story line of the origin myths of a number of early kingdoms and states, including, for example, the Aztecs of Central Mexico (Durán, 1964), the Bantu-speaking peoples of Central and East Africa (Beattie, 1960; de Heusch, 1982), and the Hawaiian and Fijiian Islanders (Sahlins, 1985). This is as well the outline of the cycle of myths to be discussed in this study, one of two great mythic cycles recorded in the Spanish chronicles from Peru between the 1540s and the 1650s concerning the origins of the Inka empire. The cycle of origin myths that I will be concerned with here focuses on the emergence of the ancestors of the Inkas from a cave at a place called Pacariqtambo (inn of dawn, or origin).[1] After their emergence at Pacariqtambo, the ancestors traveled northward to a fertile valley, where they founded the city of Cuzco, the future capital of the Inka empire.

While the image of the ancestors as strangers, or outsiders, is not unique to the Inkas, what *is* somewhat unusual about the origin place in Inka mythic history is that it is possible in this case to study the actual site of the supposed homeland of the ancestors. That is, since (as I will show here) the actual place of the emergence of the ancestors in the Pacariqtambo cycle of origin myths was associated by some of the people who recounted this story in early colonial times with a particular town and its environs (located some 26 kilometers straight south of Cuzco), it is possible, through both ethnohistorical and ethnographic study, to pursue an interpretation of the Inka origin myth from the point of view of this local community.

The aim of this study is to investigate the Inka myth of origin from the point of view of the town and region to the south of Cuzco that is known today, as it has been at least since the time of the Spanish conquest, as Pacariqtambo. I will address two central problems in this study: first, how and why did the Inka origin place become identified with—or "concretized" to—the town of Pacariqtambo? And second, what light can we shed on the political, social, and ideological foundations of the Inka state as expressed in the myth of origin on the basis of a historical and ethnographic study of the town and region of Pacariqtambo itself?

As we will find in this study, the earliest and clearest evidence to give us an insight into the processes whereby the origin place of the Inkas became identified in Spanish colonial written accounts with the modern-day town and district of Pacariqtambo is from a document that I found in the private collection of a former hacienda owner who lives near Pacariqtambo (see Appendix). The document, which dates to 1718, contains a copy of extensive testimony from a legal proceeding carried out in 1569 in which a resident of Pacariqtambo— a provincial nobleman named Rodrigo Sutiq Callapiña—successfully argued to the Spanish officials in Cuzco that he was a descendant of the first Inka king, Manqo Qhapaq. The claim by this nobleman from Pacariqtambo was supported by eight members of the Inka nobility in Cuzco, several of whom would serve shortly thereafter as witnesses in other important legal proceedings and historical investigations carried out there. Most important, several of the noblemen who testified in behalf of Rodrigo Sutiq Callapiña in 1569 later served as informants for an official history of the Inka empire, which was written by Sarmiento de Gamboa in 1572. The present study examines the intersection—in political, social, and "mythohistorical" terms—between the construction of the family history of an elite lineage in Pacariqtambo (i.e., the Callapiñas) and the writing of one of the earliest official "histories" of the empire: Sarmiento de Gamboa's *Historia de los Incas.*

It is important to point out that in addition to the myths recounting the emergence of the Inka ancestors from the cave at Pacariqtambo, there is another cycle of origin myths, which centers on Lake Titicaca and the pre-Inkaic ruins of Tiwanaku (map 1). The myths in this cycle elaborate especially the role of the deity T'iqsi Wiraqocha in the creation of the sun, the moon, and the stars, as well as the origin of humans.[2] In point of fact, these two places of origin—Pacariqtambo and Lake Titicaca—and the traditions of origin associated with them are not kept strictly separate in all accounts recorded by the Spanish chroniclers. For instance, in the chronicles written by Guaman Poma de Ayala and Murúa, we find something of a hybrid legend, which combines these two traditions of origin in the person of the ancestor-king of the empire, Manqo Qhapaq, who is said to have emerged from Lake Titicaca, from where he traveled underground to Pacariqtambo and from there on to the valley of Cuzco (Guaman Poma, 1980: ff. 80–87; Murúa, 1946:7).

Given the nature of the large, powerful, and complex chiefdom and incipient state organizations that existed around Lake Titicaca in the centuries immediately preceding the Spanish conquest (Diez de San Miguel, 1964 [1567]; Hyslop, 1979; Julien, 1982; Murra, 1975; Ramos Gavilán, 1976 [1621]), it is not surprising that the Inkas may have sought to solidify and legitimate their mandate for rule by incorporating into the foundations of their empire personages, institutions, and territorial imperatives deriving from their Aymara predecessors and contemporaries to the south. However, it would be difficult to make a similar argument in trying to explain or justify the tradition of origin myths centering on Pacariqtambo, for this community is located within a region to the south of Cuzco that is today, as it appears to have been in Inka times, something of an economic, political, and cultural backwater.

While none of the earliest versions of the Pacariqtambo cycle of origin myths, that is, those recorded from the 1540s to the 1560s, indicate where this place was located in precise geographical terms, during the period from the 1570s to the 1590s the name "Pacariqtambo" became identified in Spanish documents with a town located some 26 kilometers straight south of Cuzco. According to the Inkas' own system of imperial geopolitical classifications, Pacariqtambo was located in the hierarchically lowest quarter of the empire, the quarter known as Kuntisuyu. In late pre-Hispanic and early colonial times, Pacariqtambo was inhabited by a privileged (but

Map 1. The modern geopolitical setting of Pacariqtambo

not, apparently, more so than other elites in the circum-Cuzco region) population of Maskas Indians who were divided into some ten to twelve dispersed sociopolitical and ritual groups called *ayllus*. Therefore, although the tradition of origin centering on Pacariqtambo represents only a part of a more varied and complex body of origin myths, one might well wonder about the implications and intentions, in regional geopolitical and historical terms, of the identification of Pacariqtambo—alongside the powerful kingdoms of the Lake Titicaca region—as the origin place of the Inkas. These are some of the problems that I will address in this study.

By focusing our attention on the place of origin of the ancestors of the Inkas, rather than on the imperial city that they supposedly founded (Cuzco), we have the opportunity of "reversing," as it were, the mythical peregrinations of the ancestors in order to resituate and reexamine the structures and events of the formation of the Inka state in the local, provincial context. This strategy of investigation may not only allow us to expose a new level of meaning in the primordial events of the formation of a state, but it should also afford us a unique encounter with the age-old conundrum—the antique hall of mirrors—of the relationship between myth and history. In this regard, a few points should be clarified concerning the nature of the corpus of materials available to us for study and the presumptions that are made here with respect to the "historicity" of these materials.

Historicist and Structuralist Perspectives on the Spanish Chronicles

One of the unique features of the Inka empire, when compared with other pristine states of the Old and New worlds, is that this was one of only a few ancient states that did not develop a system of writing (if the Inkas did leave a body of written narratives, we have not yet succeeded in translating them).[3] While we are able to read Inka mathematical notations recorded in their knotted-string recording devices, called *khipus* (Ascher and Ascher, 1975, 1981), we are as yet unable to read Inka accounts of local and imperial myths and histories, if such written accounts do indeed exist in some as yet undeciphered form (e.g., in the geometrical motifs in Inka weavings, or perhaps in the *khipus* themselves). It is important to stress the point of Inka nonliteracy at the beginning of this study, because this factor has a number of general and specific consequences for the study and interpretation of the cycle of myths dealing with the origin of the Inka state at Pacariqtambo. One of the more general consequences is that we have, in fact, no true "Inka" myths. All myths and histories purporting to be Inkaic were in fact recorded by European (or European-trained) soldiers, chroniclers, and bureaucrats following the entry of the Spaniards into Peru in the early 1530s.

There is a basic difference of opinion among Andeanists concerning the historicity of pre-Hispanic dates, events, and personages mentioned in the Spanish chronicles. This difference of opinion and the radically different approaches to Andean studies resulting from it are best exemplified in the studies produced by John H. Rowe and R. Tom Zuidema.

For several decades, Rowe has approached the task of constructing an Inka culture history by means of the application of logic in the comparative analysis of the data provided in the Spanish chronicles (Rowe, 1945, 1985a, 1985b). For example, in the 1940s, Rowe, working through the "discrepancies" recorded in the various chronicles concerning the lengths of the reigns of the various Inka kings, but accepting basically the data provided in the chronicle of Cabello Valboa (1951 [1586]), proposed a series of absolute dates for the Inka kings (1945, 1946). Having thereby established a chronological framework of a single line of dynastic succession, it was possible for him to proceed with the study of Andean history and historiography in much the same way that the enterprise of history has traditionally been practiced in the West, that is, as a linear series of events built on the chronological foundation of a succession of kings. In two more recent studies Rowe has essentially reproduced the methodological and theoretical orientations on the "historicist" interpretation of the Spanish chronicles that he articulated in his earlier work (1985a, 1985b).

On the other hand, Zuidema has argued in a series of publications since the 1960s that, since we have no written records predating the arrival of the Spaniards in Peru, and therefore no indigenous, non-European (or non–European influenced) accounts of the structure, organization, and history of the Inka empire, we have no basis on which to evaluate the historicity of events recorded in the chronicles. For instance, the various accounts that are given in the chronicles concerning the Inka kings may well represent Spanish (mis-) *interpretations* of the institution of Inka kingship according to the European models of dynasties and principles of dynastic succession with which the Spaniards of the sixteenth century were very familiar. Therefore, because of the impossibility of evaluating the historicity of the material in the chronicles from an indigenous, pre-Hispanic point of view, we cannot use the data provided by the Spanish chronicles with any confidence to construct a history of the Inkas. Rather, the chronicles should be viewed, according to Zuidema, as containing intentional representations of the organization and structure of the Inka empire that were informed and motivated by various pre-Hispanic and colonial political, social, ritual, and other considerations by *both* the indigenous informants and the chroniclers themselves (1964, 1982c, 1983, 1986).

The disagreement emerging from the two positions outlined here is fundamental and leads to profoundly different statements of problems in Andean studies as well as to the formulation of strategies for their investigation. It is important to note that this debate is not unique, in theoretical terms, to Andean studies; it is found, for instance, in the controversy between "literal" (or historical) and "structural" interpretations of Indo-European myths (Dumezil, 1977 [1959]). In addition, a remarkably similar debate to that in the Andes has gone on for several decades in the study of Central African "historical" narratives. On one side, Vansina has consistently argued for literal, historical interpretations of the origin myths of kingdoms among the Bantu-speaking peoples of Central Africa; one example is the Luba epic of the founding of the kingdom of Katanga (Vansina, 1965:55–56, cited in de Heusch, 1982:9). In a brief review of the debate between Vansina and J. C. Miller on the historicity of this (and related) origin myths, Willis concludes that Vansina's position was effectively undermined when Miller demonstrated "that *Kinguri* [a central character in the epic whose death leads to the emergence of divine kingship] was not a historical individual but the name of a titled office transmitted down the generations by a common Central African procedure known to anthropologists as 'positional succession.' Consequently, there was no basis for Vansina's dating of the Lunda state's foundation to 'just before 1600' (de Heusch, 1982:xi).

The debate in Central African studies, which is seen in the opposition between literalist and structuralist interpretations of origin myths, is strikingly similar to one in Andean studies concerning the historicity of the pre-Hispanic kings of the Inka dynasty (or dynasties). That is, Rowe has argued that, while the first eight kings of the Inka empire are shadowy, we can be relatively certain of the historicity as well as the dates of the reign of the ninth king, Pachakuti Inka—A.D. 1438–1471 (Rowe, 1945:273, 277; 1946:203; 1985a:35; see also Niles, 1987:7). Zuidema's position with respect not only to Pachakuti Inka, but to all of the kings who supposedly ruled before the arrival of the Spaniards, is that each name was, in fact, a *title* in a complex dualistic and hierarchical structure of genealogical and administrative positions (1983:50–53; 1986:64–66). The elaborations of this imperial (mythohistorical) administrative structure by native informants in the years immediately following the conquest were transformed by the Spanish chroniclers into a European-style, linear chronology by the representation of this system of hereditary titles, a system perhaps similar to "positional succession," as a single line of dynastic succession (see also Duviols, 1979b, 1980; Wedin, 1963).

We should elaborate here on the nature of African systems of "positional succession" as these relate to particular models of history; these data will help to clarify further the distinction between the historicist and structuralist approaches to the Spanish chronicles. In a study of the tribal organization of the Mambwe of Northern Rhodesia, Watson describes the Mambwe system of positional succession as follows:

> All Mambwe titles stand in perpetual relationship to that of
> NSOKOLO, the senior title, and to each other, irrespective of the
> actual genealogical relationships between the living incumbents.
> The actual genealogical relationships between individuals are ir-
> relevant in the context of titles and political authority.
> When the incumbent of a title dies, his successor assumes his
> title and authority, and at the same time, his exact place in the
> kinship system. He takes on the complete social identity of his
> predecessor and inherits his wives, children, and property, in ad-
> dition to the title. . . .
> The consistency of the [Mambwe] genealogies arises, I believe,
> because they are statements of the political relationships be-
> tween living people who occupy enduring positions, and not the
> remembered precise relationships between actual dead or liv-
> ing people. Mambwe genealogies record not only the descent of
> persons, but also the descent of titles and estates. (Watson,
> 1964:145, 150)

The important point to stress for our purposes concerning the nature of history as it will be shaped in the context of a political organization like the Mambwe system of positional succession (which may be similar in some respects to the organization of bureaucratic offices and the system of dynastic succession in the Inka state) is that the events that are associated with particular titles (e.g., the names of the Inka kings) are not, by their nature, *chronological;* rather, "events" are elaborations of the status, duties, and so on, associated with various positions in a hierarchical political organization. When the Spaniards began investigating the Inka system of political organization in the mid-sixteenth century, they misunderstood the essentially political, rather than chronological, nature of the "historical events" recounted by their native informants. Thus, the chroniclers misrepresented political structures as chronological events, and in the process they effectively historicized what was, at the base of it, an ideology of history that was timeless, repetitive, and fully interchangeable—and integrated—with political, social, and ritual structure.

I will return to such questions as the historicizing of the Inka origin myth and of the Inka kings, as well as a consideration of the role played in these processes by an important and influential descendant of the lineage of Pachakuti Inka, in chapter 3.

As will become apparent, I essentially accept the structural—or better, *mytho*historical—approach to the interpretation of the Spanish chronicles. My basic reasons for accepting this position are, first, that since all any one of the chroniclers had as a basis for constructing a history of the empire were the memories of informants and the observation of the remnants of the empire that lay in tatters around him, it does not seem reasonable to suppose that a source existed for constructing a "true," unmotivated history of the empire (either at the level of the simple occurrence of any particular event, or at the level of the chronological sequence of all events reported in any particular chronicle). Second, to begin the interpretation of Inka cultural and social history with the notion that a true version of that history exists—a dubious proposition in itself—encourages the systematic rephrasing of the many *differences* that one encounters in the various accounts in the chronicles as *discrepancies;* this leads in turn to the (in my opinion) short-sighted notion that the work of Andean history and historiography is about resolving discrepancies (e.g., by choosing one account over others) rather than about trying to understand and explain why and how different chroniclers, perhaps using different informants or different classes of informants, might have arrived at fundamentally different interpretations of Inka history. The latter would seem to present us with the most creative approach in that it allows for and encourages the construction of a number of "approximations" of Andean *histories,* each incorporating and reflecting a point of view held on the Inka past by different individuals and groups involved in representing that past to the Spanish chroniclers. The present study will show, in fact, the role of certain individuals and of certain *types* of individuals (i.e., Inka noblemen and provincial elites), in the motivated construction of particular representations of the origin of the Inkas from Pacariqtambo.

In summary, my own views on the nature of pre-Hispanic history in the Andes are similar to those expressed by Ohnuki-Tierney in a study of symbolic transformations in Japanese history and ritual:

As we [anthropologists] have begun to confront historical processes, somewhat ironically we have also become aware that history "in the raw" was an erroneously held ideal in the past; we do not simply "reconstruct" history from "objective facts" recorded in archives. We are fully aware that both ethnographic and historical representations are incomplete, partial, and over-determined by forces such as the inequalities of power—the forces that are beyond the control or consciousness of the individuals who are involved in the complex process of representing and interpreting the "other," be it historical or ethnographic. (1987:3)

Political Hierarchies and the Postconquest Control of Inka History

Although there is not, to my knowledge, a single example in which the archaeological record in the Andes ties a particular *event* recorded by the Spaniards in one of the purported histories of the Inka empire to an absolute date in pre-Hispanic chronology (e.g., the accession of a king to the throne; the waging of a particular war; or the relocation of an ethnic group from one part of the empire to another), the stories recorded in the Spanish chronicles are nonetheless of central importance for the interpretation of both pre-Hispanic and postconquest societies in the Andes. The reasons for this are, first, the stories recorded in the early colonial documents as told by native informants are the closest things we have to indigenous, non–European influenced testimonies of the nature and state of affairs of societies in the Andes in pre-Hispanic times; and second, this body of lore formed the basis on which Andean peoples began to construct and reinterpret their own past. These versions, representing the majority of the materials recorded in the Spanish chronicles, were constructed in the context of the new realities and hierarchical relationships of the early colonial world (i.e., from the mid-1500s to the mid-1600s).

Therefore, the stories recorded in the chronicles that are set in pre-Hispanic times can be regarded as myths or legends from which a literary tradition of "official histories" began to emerge in the first few decades following the Spanish invasion. These written accounts became the vehicles for concretizing and historicizing Inka mythology (see Adorno, 1986; MacCormack, 1984, 1985; Rostworowski, 1983:99–106; Zamora, 1988). Because of the ambiguous—mythical/historical—status of the material in these documents, I will refer here to all stories recorded in the Spanish chronicles that describe pre-Hispanic (i.e., pre-1532) events, persons, places, and the like, as "mythohistories."[4]

The implications for our specific study of the absence of primary (pre-Hispanic) accounts of clearly discernible Inka myths and histories are threefold. In the first place, the mythohistorical traditions preserved in the chronicles are the products of at least two stages of representation and interpretation, one on the part of the person recounting the story, the other on the part of the person recording it. When a translator entered the process to render the narrative from Quechua into Spanish, another level of interpretation was added. Thus, the Inka mythohistorical traditions preserved in the Spanish chronicles are the product of variously motivated, hierarchical interpretations (i.e., teller → translator → recorder). The possibility of ambiguities, misunderstandings, and individually motivated interpretations entering the accounts throughout this process is enormous.

The second point is actually a corollary to the first; that is, the myths recorded in the chronicles were collected in a conquest setting. The storyteller was in virtually all instances subordinate to the listener/recorder. This state of affairs brings up questions such as the following: Does one tell the same story of one's origins to the conqueror as one might have told previously to the conquered? What advantage might be gained in a conquest setting by emphasizing certain points in a story and perhaps omitting others? Or of changing the story altogether to cast one's self or one's own lineage or social group in a more favorable light?

The third observation on the manner in which Inka mythohistory was (re)constructed by, and for, the Spaniards concerns the hierarchical point of view of the testimony. Hierarchy was a central, organizing principle of relations in virtually all areas of life in pre-Hispanic Andean societies. The hierarchical character of Inka sociopolitical institutions produced and sustained a conquest society whose empire incorporated a remarkable range and diversity of ethnic groups and environments. The bureaucratic systems through which these institutions were articulated and affairs of state were managed were similarly hierarchically organized, from officials governing ten households to those governing forty thousand. With the Spanish conquest, the imperial, regional, and local hierarchies of authority and governance collapsed. Nonetheless, it was within the context of that recent history of a hierarchically structured society that the new colonial society, as well as the historicized representations of the Inka past, began to take shape.

The questions that are of interest with respect to these observations are, first, who had the privilege of representing to the Spanish the history of the Inka empire? And second, what were the consequences for people both inside the imperial city of Cuzco as well as for those outside—in places like Pacariqtambo—of the exercise of this privilege? It is clear that inside Cuzco, accounts of the history of the empire were constructed by the Spanish overwhelmingly on the basis of the testimony provided by (male) members of the Inka nobility. We will find in this study that in the provincial community of Pacariqtambo, history, particularly as it concerned the origin of the Inkas, was the product of the testimony of descendants of the local elites, but more particularly of one especially powerful and long-lived lineage of *caciques principales* (high-level local officials), the Callapiña family.

The highly interpretive and hierarchical nature of Inka mytho-history provides the rationale for going beyond the apparent content and structure of the myths that were told about the Inkas by their postconquest descendants to a consideration of some of the local political, social, and even geographical features that are "embedded" within those myths. In this study of the cycle of myths concerning the origin of the Inkas as seen from the point of view of Pacariq-tambo, I will show that such special technical and local information was indeed known to at least some of the narrators and that it undoubtedly constituted a part of the nonverbalized motivation behind particular characteristics that certain versions of this myth contain.

Therefore, what I propose to do in this study is to "step between" some of the people who told certain versions of the Inka origin myth and others who recorded them some three or four centuries ago in order to supply some of the local information that may have constituted a level of representation and interpretation in the myths to which individual storytellers had access, but which was almost assuredly unknown to the Spanish listeners. It was the knowledge of, and the ability to use, such specialized, technical geographical and political information (whose most meaningful referents lay within the recent pre-Hispanic past) that constituted the principal tactic used by elites throughout the empire in their attempts to exert some measure of control and, in many cases, to advance their own positions in the increasingly historicized representations of the Inka past that were recorded in the Spanish chronicles. Emerging out of this process as well was what I will refer to here as the "concretization" of the place of origin, that is, the identification of the origin place—in the case at hand, Pacariqtambo—in unambiguous toponyms. I would emphasize that this localization of mythic space appears to have resulted from the Spanish drive to historicize Inka mytho-history for administrative and bureaucratic purposes, rather than from a desire on the part of the natives to delimit, and in the process conflate, mythic space and political geography within the circum-Cuzco region.

The bases on which I propose to construct a Pacariqtambo-centered point of view on, or reading of, the representation and interpretation of the origin myth through time are the following. First, I carried out some thirty months of ethnographic fieldwork in and around the modern-day town of Pacariqtambo between 1980 and 1988. During this time, I became reasonably familiar with the geography of this place, with its contemporary inhabitants, and with their forms of social, economic, and ritual organization (Urton, 1984, 1985 *a*, 1985 *b*, 1986, 1988, *n.d.a*, *n.d.b.*). And second, during this time of study, I also transcribed several hundred pages of historical documents pertaining to Pacariqtambo from collections in both public and private archives in Peru. These experiences and data will allow us to take a unique perspective on the Inka origin myth, particularly when compared to earlier studies, which have interpreted the myth primarily from an imperial, Cuzqueñan point of view.

The contrast between an imperial and a provincial perspective on the interpretation of the origin myth can be demonstrated most clearly by recounting the central storyline of the cycle of myths in question and then pointing out how a local, Pacariqtambo interpretation of the myth can enrich and augment the imperial Cuzqueñan perspective.

An Outline of the Inka Origin Myth

In outline form, and paraphrasing several versions of the myth, especially that contained in Sarmiento de Gamboa's *Historia de los Incas* (1942 [1572]: 49–59), to be considered in detail in chapter 2, the origin myth tells the following story:

At a place to the south of Cuzco called Pacariqtambo, there is a mountain called Tampu T'oqo (window house) in which there are three windows, or caves. At the beginning of time, a group of four brothers and their four sisters—the ancestors of the Inkas— emerged from the central window. The principal figure of this group was Manqo Qhapaq, the man who was destined to become the founder-king of the empire. One of the first acts of the eight ancestors was to organize the people who were living around Tampu T'oqo into ten groups, called *ayllus*. The full entourage of ancestral siblings and *ayllus* set off from Tampu T'oqo to the north in search of fertile land on which to build their imperial capital, Cuzco. Along the way, they stopped at several places to test the soil. At one of these stops, Manqo Qhapaq and one of his sisters, Mama Oqllu, conceived a child whom they named Sinchi Ruq'a. After a period of wanderings filled with marvelous events the entourage arrived at a hill overlooking the valley of Cuzco.

Recognizing by miraculous signs that this was their long-sought-after home, the Inkas descended from the mountain and took possession of the valley.

This, in the barest of forms, is the gist of the Inka origin myth, which begins at Pacariqtambo and ends at Cuzco. In most studies of this myth, the perspective taken in the analysis of the events of the origin myth is "Cuzco-centric" in the sense that they explore the relevance of the characters, events, and structures of the myth as prefigurations, or reflexive commentaries, on imperial Cuzqueñan mythohistory. These analyses focus on such points as the characteristics and "functions" of the ancestral group of brothers and sisters in imperial ideology and mythology (e.g., Urbano, 1980, 1981); the place of the ten *ayllus* that were formed at Pacariqtambo in the sociopolitical and ritual organizations of the city of Cuzco (e.g., Rostworowski, 1983; Rowe, 1985a; Zuidema, 1964, 1986); and other such "post-Pacariqtambo," imperial concerns.

My point here is not to criticize these studies, but rather to contrast these approaches with that to be taken here, an approach that will focus explicitly on the relevance of the structures and events described in the origin myth from the perspective of Pacariqtambo. The analytical point of view proposed here is unique because by emphasizing a provincial, rather than an imperial, point of view, it places in the foreground a potentially entirely different set of considerations from those of the empire as a whole. For instance, this point of view will encourage us to investigate such questions as the following: What does the origin myth suggest about the nature of early colonial social and political organizations in and around Pacariqtambo at the time these myths were recorded in Cuzco (i.e., from the 1540s to the early 1600s)? What does the origin myth imply about the nature of relations and interactions between the political center (Cuzco) and a peripheral community (Pacariqtambo) in both pre- and early postconquest times? And most important for our study, how did the people of Pacariqtambo view and use this mythohistorical tradition, which cast their community in a privileged light, in the context of the institutions and relationships of early colonial Peru?

We will find that residents of Pacariqtambo from the sixteenth through the eighteenth centuries were indeed aware of the identification of their village as the origin place of the Inkas, that they were active participants in the construction of that tradition, and that they used it to their advantage on every possible occasion. The last will become especially clear when we examine the record of claims made by certain members of the Callapiña family for recognition of their noble status and, therefore, the award of special privileges and exemptions in the colonial taxation system by virtue of the fact that they were in a direct line of descent from the first Inka king, Manqo Qhapaq. The stakes of the concretization, or localization, of the origin place for people in Pacariqtambo were very high indeed, and the history that we will trace in the local manipulations of this imperial mythohistorical tradition is one of individual and family struggles to gain power and privilege.

Historical and Ethnographic Perspectives on Inka Mythohistory

To the degree to which this study is motivated by the experience of having lived in Pacariqtambo and of having thought about and talked to the residents of this community about their own perceptions of themselves and their past, this study may be viewed as a "partisan" history. That is, the particular, provincial point of view adopted here in the interpretation of the Inka origin myth is not merely a methodological exercise, "to see how it looks from the other way around," but rather, it assumes the position that one is given this provincial, "outside" point of view by birth or other historical circumstances and that under those circumstances, the provincial point of view is the proper, if not the only available, point of view to take in the construction of history.

In addition, in its overall organization and presentation of data this study will take into account social, political, and ritual structures and practices in the community of Pacariqtambo from colonial through contemporary times (chapter 4). Such an enterprise is undertaken at the risk of a misunderstanding arising that Andean communities are conceived to have remained encapsulated in time, untouched by history, from early colonial times to the present. It is assumed here, to the contrary, that Andean history from the sixteenth century to the present is a record of trauma and transformation. That is, we should recognize from the beginning that there are no "innocent survivors"—institutions and practices untouched by history—in the Andes. That an institution or practice bears the name of what appears to be a similar institution or practice recorded in Inka mythohistory does not necessarily mean that there exists a continuity of structure, function, or context of action between the two examples. Any similarities between the two should be viewed rather as the subjects for analysis, taking into account the widest possible range of circumstances and contexts in which the institutions were acted on, or the practices performed, in their respective eras.

Of course, one can avoid the risk of provoking such misunderstandings by pursuing a form of social analysis that remains within the premodern, historical time frame and simply disregarding contemporary Andean peoples and societies. However, this course of action, whether taken out of caution or ignorance or lack of experience of life in a modern Andean community, is tantamount to the disenfranchisement of Andean peoples from their own history and a denial of the value and validity of their interpretations of, and action on, that history. I hope to show here that we can considerably enrich our understanding of ideologies of history in the Andes by incorporating information on the contemporary practices and historical perspectives of people in Andean communities today. Therefore, this study will take into account the points of view, interpretations, and practices of people and sociopolitical groups (i.e., the *ayllus*) in Pacariqtambo in the analysis of the Inka origin myth.[5]

Finally, I would point out that it is not the purpose of this study to historicize the *content* of the cycle of origin myths centering on Pacariqtambo, for our investigation will in no respect diminish the fabulous and richly symbolic character of this mythohistorical tradition. Rather, my aim here is to explore the individual and collective social and political processes underlying the creation of historicized *representations* of the origin myth and the uses to which those representations were put, beginning in the years immediately following the Spanish conquest of Peru.

A brief outline of the organization of this book will perhaps be of use to the reader in finding his or her way through the work. Chapter 2 provides background information on the content of different versions of the Inka origin myth, especially that in the chronicle of Sarmiento de Gamboa. This information is essential to understanding the arguments that are made in the remainder of the book. Chapter 3 examines a number of sixteenth-century documents that were important milestones in the early construction of historicized representations of Inka mythohistory. This chapter includes discussions of the document concerning the history of the Callapiña family (alluded to earlier) as well as an examination of the identities of some of the informants who testified on behalf of the Callapiñas and, somewhat later, for Sarmiento de Gamboa. Chapter 4 presents ethnographic and ethnohistorical information on the social and geopolitical organizations of populations in the area of Pacariqtambo today and in the middle to latter part of the sixteenth century. This chapter provides the essential data for a local interpretation of the structures and events described in the origin myth. Chapter 5 then sets these local structures in motion by examining ritual practices in the area of Pacariqtambo today; these data provide the basis for reflecting on the structures and events described in the Inka origin myth, particularly as they pertain to interactions among groups within Pacariqtambo and between Pacariqtambo and Cuzco. Chapter 6, the concluding chapter, presents an interpretation of the Inka origin myth from the perspective of Pacariqtambo.

2. The Pacariqtambo Origin Myth in the Spanish Chronicles

To address the questions posed in chapter 1 concerning the concretization of the Inka origin place and the historicizing of Inka mythohistory in the Spanish chronicles, it is necessary to describe and elaborate on a number of the structures, institutions, and principles of organization that are placed at Pacariqtambo at the beginning of time. These descriptions will provide the materials necessary for our later discussion of social and territorial organizations in and around Pacariqtambo during the sixteenth century as these were described in local documents dating from about the same time that information on the origin myth was being recorded by the Spanish in Cuzco.

There are some forty versions of the cycle of myths with which we are concerned—what Urbano (1981) refers to as "the mythic cycle of the *Ayares:* origins of the Indians and of the Incas" recorded in the Spanish chronicles over the period from 1542 to 1653.[1] It is impossible (and unnecessary) to reproduce all of the information in those accounts here. Instead, relying on the synopsis given in chapter 1 for the storyline of the myths of the origin of the Inkas from Pacariqtambo, I will expand on certain key elements in this outline. The three key elements—by which I mean those events that occur in or around Pacariqtambo in the origin myth that set the stage for the founding of the empire—include the following: (1) the emergence of the eight ancestors from the cave of origin; (2) the ancestors' creation of ten *ayllus;* and (3) the events that transpired at various places along the route as the ancestors and *ayllus* traveled from Pacariqtambo to Cuzco.

The principal account that I will use in elaborating these elements is that given in Sarmiento de Gamboa's *Historia de los Incas* (1942 [1572]: 49–59). Sarmiento's account is one of the earliest and most detailed versions that we have. As the official historian to Viceroy Francisco de Toledo, Sarmiento had access to an unusually large number of informants; he interviewed more than one hundred *khipu-kamayuqs* (recordkeepers) who had served the Incas as historians before the time of the conquest. In what is perhaps one of the most grandiloquent assertions of veracity and trustworthiness in all of Andean historiography, Sarmiento concludes his account with an epilogue in which he goes to great lengths to establish the undeniable truth and historicity of his chronicle. He says that he had his chronicle read in full, in the native Quechua language, to a group of forty-two descendants of the Inka nobility. All of these men, Sarmiento says, agreed that "the said history was good and true and conformed to what they knew and to what they had heard their parents and ancestors say, which they themselves had heard their own [parents and ancestors] say" (Sarmiento, 1942 [1572]:180; unless otherwise noted, all translations are mine).

I do not mean to suggest by my reliance on Sarmiento, nor by my repetition of its assertions of trustworthiness, that we are to accept his history as true "history," at least not in the sense in which that term is often opposed to "myth." Rather, Sarmiento's account is important because it incorporates the points of view of some of the noble descendants of each of the kings who supposedly ruled the empire before the Spanish conquest of Peru. Therefore, Sarmiento de Gamboa's account allows us to study in some detail the political and social contexts of the production of at least one early version of the origin myth. In addition, Sarmiento's account contains certain topographical information concerning the location of the place known as Pacariqtambo, which suggests that at least one of his informants was familiar with the actual geography of the region known by this name today. In fact, it appears to be in Sarmiento's account that "Pacariqtambo," which had been represented in the chronicles written before this time as something of a generic "place of origin" (*paqarina*), and whose location was not precisely defined, became concretized to a specific town and its environs to the south of the valley of Cuzco. Why at least some of Sarmiento's informants in 1572 delimited the space of the Inka place of origin in their testimony is one of the central problems that we will address later in this study (chapter 3).

The Emergence of the Ancestral Siblings/Spouses from the Cave of Tampu T'oqo

At the beginning of his account, Sarmiento de Gamboa says that the origin of the Inkas was a place called Pacaritambo (the inn of dawn; or place of origin), a name that he glosses as "the house of production." Sarmiento says that Pacariqtambo (Pacaritambo) was located "six leagues [ca. 33 kilometers] to the south-southwest of Cuzco."[2] (The modern-day town of Pacariqtambo is located 26 kilometers straight south of Cuzco.) At Pacariqtambo there was a mountain called Tampu T'oqo (Tambotoco, "the house of windows") in which were located three "windows"; elsewhere, the windows are referred to as "caves" (e.g., Polo de Ondegardo, 1916 [1571]: 53; Murúa, 1946 [1590]: 6). The central window of the group of three windows was called Qhapaq T'oqo (Capac-toco, "rich window") and the two lateral windows were called Maras T'oqo (Maras-toco) and Sutiq T'oqo (Sutic-toco). At the beginning of time, a nation of Indians called the Maras emerged from the window of Maras T'oqo. Another group of people, the Tambos, emerged from Sutiq T'oqo. Sarmiento says that at the time of writing his account, there were still members of both the Maras and Tambos ethnic groups living in Cuzco (Sarmiento, 1942 [1572]: 49).

From the central window—Qhapaq T'oqo—at Tampu T'oqo there emerged four men and four women who were, according to Sarmiento, brothers and sisters.[3] The ancestral siblings had neither father nor mother; rather, they were born from the window of Qhapaq T'oqo at the urging, or the command, of T'iqsi Wiraqocha (Sarmiento, 1942 [1572]: 49). The title "T'iqsi Wiraqocha" (or, as written by Sarmiento, "Ticci Viracocha") is often translated as "creator-god." However, this title is probably best glossed in the context of the origin myth as "founder of the lineage," or "father of the *ayllus* of the ethnic group" (Duviols, 1977: 59).

Sarmiento next gives the names of the eight ancestral siblings. It is important in naming the ancestors to retain the order in which Sarmiento enumerates them, because he lists the two groups—first, that of the four brothers and then that of the four sisters—in parallel hierarchical rankings. The brothers, Sarmiento says, were ranked by authority, the sisters by age (1942 [1572]: 49). The ancestors are identified in table 1.

Sarmiento does not elaborate on the nature or source of the "authority" by which the four brothers were ranked hierarchically. As described in the origin myth, it seems as though the "natural" age-based hierarchy of the ancestral women provided the model for the political ranking among their brothers. This principle of hierarchical ranking will reappear later when we discuss the social organization of Inka Cuzco. In Cuzco, the ranking among the age grades of the female nobility may have provided the basis for the hierarchical ranking among the ten social groups of the nobility (the royal *ayllus*, or *panaqas*) of the city. Therefore, Sarmiento's informants seem to

Table 1. *The Ancestors of the Inkas*

Brothers	Sisters
Manqo Qhapaq	Mama Oqllu
Ayar Awka	Mama Waku
Ayar Kachi	Mama Ipakura/Kura
Ayar Uchu	Mama Rawa

Note: The names of the ancestors may be glossed as follows (Bertonio, 1984; González Holguín, 1952; Urbano, 1981):

Ayar Manqho: "first ancestor" (Ayar is probably from *aya*, "corpse").
Manqo Qhapaq: "first rich [ancestor]."
Ayar Awka: "ancestor enemy."
Ayar Kachi: "ancestor salt."
Ayar Uchu: "ancestor chile pepper."
Mama Oqllu: "shapely [plump] mother."
Mama Waku: "cheek [jaw] mother"; "grandmother."
Mama Ipakura: "maternal aunt/daughter-in-law castration mother."
Mama Rawa: "[?] mother."

have identified birth order, linked by siblingship to a hierarchy of authority, as the primordial set of organizational principles and relationships in Inka mythohistory.

The principle of age as a basis for ranking is found in a somewhat different form in Betanzos's earlier (1551) version of the origin myth. Betanzos says that the ancestors were paired as spouses; the pairs were related to each other in a kind of birth order, based on the successive emergence of four couples from the cave of Tampu T'oqo. Betanzos says that the first couple to emerge was Ayar Kachi and his wife Mama Waku; then came Ayar Uchu and [Mama] Kura; next came Ayar Awka and Rawa Oqllu; and finally Ayar Manqo, "who was later called Manqo Qhapaq," and his wife Mama Oqllu (1968 [1551]:11–12). While the various accounts of the origin myth may identify the ancestors either as siblings, spouses, or both, in all cases the links represent consanguineal or affinal ties within a *single* generation.

Therefore, in its initial stage, the origin myth is concerned primarily with the problem of defining the status of political ranking in relation to categories, or groups, classified on the basis of age and gender. In the next section I shall describe how the origin myth projects these primordial relations into the foundation of imperial society in the form of a moiety system composed of ten hierarchically ranked sociopolitical and ritual groups, called *ayllus*. It is important to elaborate on these descriptions of the relations and organization of the ancestors and the *ayllus* that were created at Tampu T'oqo because these data will form the base on which we will later compare the representations of the composition and organization of sociopolitical groups in the area of Pacariqtambo as portrayed in the origin myth and those that actually existed in this area as described in local historical documents dating from the 1560s to the 1590s.

The Origin of *Ayllus*

After the emergence of the eight ancestors, conflict, driven by greed and the will to conquer neighboring peoples, appeared. Society was formed out of this primordial conflict and the belligerence that motivated it. That is, immediately upon their emergence from Tampu T'oqo, the eight ancestors began stirring up trouble by saying that they were strong and wise and that they were going to join the Tambos Indians who lived around Tampu T'oqo and go in search of fertile land. They said that when they found it, they would conquer and subdue the people who lived there. These bellicose statements were made by Mama Waku and Manqo Qhapaq, both of whom were said to be especially fierce and cruel. Sarmiento describes this turn of events as follows: "And agreeing among themselves on this [plan for conquest], the eight [ancestors] began to stir up the people who lived in that part of the mountain, setting as the prize that they [the ancestors] would make them rich and that they would give them the lands and estates that they conquered and subjugated. From an interest in this [proposition], there were formed ten parts or *ayllos*, which means, among these barbarians, a lineage or faction" (Sarmiento, 1942 [1572]: 50).

Before discussing the ten *ayllus* (*ayllos*) that were formed among the Tambos Indians who lived around Tampu T'oqo, it will be helpful to look at the general meanings and applications of the Quechua word *ayllu* as it is used in Inka and present-day Quechua kinship and sociopolitical organization.

In general terms, the word *ayllu* refers to a "group," or unit, of social, political, economic, and ritual cohesion and action. Examples of *ayllu* could include a state, an ethnic group within a state, a residentially localized faction within an ethnic group, a kindred, the people sharing an irrigation canal, or groups formed to celebrate festivals or to undertake work projects. The term is glossed in various

historical sources as "band," "faction," or "lineage" (González Holguín, 1952 [1608]: 39; Sarmiento, 1942 [1572]: 50). Sarmiento uses
the terms *"cuadrillas"* (groups) and *"parcialidades"* (parts of a whole)
as apparent synonyms of *ayllu*. From descriptions of *ayllus* in documents beginning with the colonial period and continuing to the
present day, it is clear that whether grounded in kinship, territo-
riality, labor organization, or some other principle, *ayllus* are basic
units, or categories, in Quechua classificatory practice. As such, the
concept of *"ayllu"* is closely synonymous with our terms "genus,"
"species," and "type" (González Holguín, 1952 [1608]: 39–40; see
Urton, 1985*a*: 278–279).

With respect to the more general, classificatory sense in which
this term may be used, it is interesting to note for comparative purposes that *ayllu* appears to have a remarkably similar status and
range of meanings to the Ilongot (northern Luzon, Philippines) word
bertan. For example, in the following quotation, which comes from
Rosaldo's description of Ilongot social organization (1980: 222), one
can, without doing too much violence to the cultural integrity of the
Andean side of the equation, substitute the Quechua word *ayllu* for
the Ilongot word *bertan*.

> The word *bertan* ranges in meaning from an all-purpose classi-
> fier to a designation for groups of people. In its broader sense
> *bertan* is a classifier par excellence. It can apply to virtually any-
> thing that can be enumerated. Most things in this world, includ-
> ing animals, people, and words, are said in their diversity to be of
> many *bertan*.
>
> In a narrower yet related sense, the term *bertan* can be used as
> a category of affiliation to designate a group of people. . . . The
> term so employed refers to a particular kind of people, especially
> as contrasted with another such kind.

On the basis of her fieldwork in the village of Chuschi (Depart-
ment of Ayacucho), Isbell has defined the term *"ayllu"* as "any
group with a head" (Isbell, 1977). This definition presupposes a hierarchical relation within the *ayllu*, and that is the general nature of
ayllus as they are described in both the historical and the ethnographic literature. The boundary between the inside and the outside
of an *ayllu* is usually mediated by a category of allied individuals or
groups often composed of (or classified as) affines. The boundary
group mediating relations between an *ayllu* and outsiders is often
designated by the affinal kin term *"qatay"* (brother-in-law/son-
in-law) and, on occasion, *"qachun"* (sister-in-law/daughter-in-law;

see Allen, 1984:159–162; Isbell, 1977:100; Poole, 1984:141; Skar, 1982:189–197; Urton, n.d.b.; Zuidema, 1977:260–263, 1986:36–38). The asymmetrical relations between *ayllu* members and those included within the boundary group constitute one of the bases (another of which is the relation between seniors and juniors) for the formation and maintenance of hierarchical relations within *ayllu* groupings.

In Sarmiento's account of the Inka origin myth, the primary motivation underlying the formation of the first *ayllus* was a desire to gain land and wealth; conquest is represented as the means for achieving these ends. Therefore, from the point of view of Sarmiento's informants in the 1570s, the first *ayllus* were territorial and political groups whose primordial concerns were the exercise of power in the pursuit of prestige and the accumulation of land. This would not be an inappropriate characterization of the nature and function of *ayllus* in Andean communities from early colonial times to the present, although it by no means exhausts the characteristics ascribed to these groups in the ethnographic literature (see Allen, 1984, 1988; Isbell, 1977, 1985).

After describing the origin of *ayllus*, Sarmiento identifies the ten such groups that were formed among the people who lived around the mountain of Tampu T'oqo at the time of the creation. As in his enumeration of the eight ancestors into one group of four brothers and another of four sisters, Sarmiento lists the ten *ayllus* in two groups of five *ayllus* each; the first group of five is identified as composing the moiety of Hanancuzco (upper Cuzco), the second group as composing that of *Hurincuzco* (lower Cuzco). The names of the ten *ayllus* are listed in their moiety groupings in table 2.

Shortly after their creation, the *ayllus* traveled to Cuzco with the eight ancestors, where they were destined to form the basis for the social, political, and ritual organization of the non-Inkaic populations who lived within the Cuzco valley (Sarmiento, 1942 [1572]: 50–51).[4] Sarmiento says that in his time, the descendants of the ten *ayllus* that were created at Pacariqtambo all lived in a section of Cuzco called Cayocache; Sarmiento identified Cayocache with the parish of Belén (Sarmiento, 1942 [1572]:51). Belén is located where the foot trail (an old Inka road) and the modern truck road enter Cuzco from the south, the direction from Cuzco to Pacariqtambo.

As a full consideration of the role of the ten *ayllus* in the political organization of Inka Cuzco is beyond the scope of this study (see Zuidema, 1964, 1986; Rowe, 1985a), I will confine my discussion of this material to two topics. The first concerns the moiety organization; the second concerns a discussion of those *ayllus* that are espe-

Table 2. *The* **Ayllus** *Founded at Pacariqtambo/Tampu T'oqo*

Hanancuzco	Hurincuzco
Chawin Cuzco Ayllu	Sutiq-T'oqo Ayllu
Arayraka Ayllu Cuzco-Kallan	Maras Ayllu
Tarpuntay Ayllu	Kuykusa Ayllu
Wakaytaqui Ayllu	Maska Ayllu
Sañuq Ayllu	Oro Ayllu

cially closely identified with Pacariqtambo either in Sarmiento's account or in other historical documents.

Before continuing, however, it should be stressed that, with respect to its identification of the ten *ayllus* created at Tampu T'oqo, Sarmiento's account is unique among the chronicles that were written up to 1572. Of the fifteen or so accounts of the origin of the Inkas that were compiled before 1572, several identify the ancestors by name, but none say anything about the creation of ten *ayllus* at Tampu T'oqo. This is also the case for those chronicles written after Sarmiento's time, with the exception of Toledo, who mentions three *ayllus* (Sauasiray, Antasayac, and Ayarucho; Toledo 1920 [1572–1575]:132–143).[5] Therefore, on the surface at least, it seems that with his one hundred *Khipukamayuq* informants, Sarmiento may have had access to a heretofore unparalleled body of information on Inka mythohistory.[6]

Sarmiento does not elaborate on the basis of the moiety division among the ten *ayllus* created at Tampu T'oqo. The moieties seem to be prefigured in the origin myth in the earlier dual division between the ancestral siblings (or spouses). If this was the case, then we may suggest, in turn, that the moieties may have been thought of by Sarmiento's informants in terms of two interrelated hierarchies, one based on age, the other on authority. (In the context of Sarmiento's chronicle, the moieties were of course more concretely "prefigured" in the sense that they were the projections into the mythic past of the moiety system of which his Cuzqueñan informants in the 1570s were a part.)

Not only does the moiety organization of the ten *ayllus* build on the dual division of the ancestors, but it also amplifies further the system of hierarchical ranking of the ancestors by adding a fifth category, or rank, to each moiety. The fifth *ayllus* of the moieties represent the incorporation of low-prestige outsiders into the imperial sociopolitical and territorial organizations. That is, Sañuq, the fifth *ayllu* of Hanancuzco, was composed of people who lived in

Sañu (modern-day San Sebastian), a town located within the valley of Cuzco, but a few kilometers to the southeast of the city. The name of the fifth *ayllu* of Hurincuzco, Oro, may be a Spanish corruption (*oro* means gold) of the Aymara word *uru*. Uru was used to designate both the pre-Inkaic, autochthonous population of the valley of Cuzco and lower-class people within the city in general.[7]

Uru was also the name of an ethnic group of fishermen and agriculturalists who lived around Lake Titicaca (Rowe, 1985a:41; Zuidema, 1964:100–101). The Uru of the Lake Titicaca region are often represented in colonial documents as brutish and contemptible people (Wachtel, 1986:283). It is interesting to note that in the organization of *ayllus* in the town of Copacabana, which lay on the shores of Lake Titicaca, there was a group called Uru Ayllu. This group, which was the fifth *ayllu* of the upper moiety in Copacabana, was also referred to as *sullka* (youngest, least) *ayllu* (Zuidema, 1964:100, n. 58). Thus, "Uru" seems to have designated low-status (e.g., junior) groupings of people in a variety of geopolitical contexts. Finally, it is no doubt more than coincidental that the extreme outer and lower group within the moiety system of Cuzco—Uru *ayllu*— implied a connection between the nonroyal *ayllus* of the valley of Cuzco and an ethnic group located at the other site (aside from Pacariqtambo), which was commonly identified as the origin place of the Inka empire—Lake Titicaca.

Athough composed of supposedly ancient, autochthonous peoples, the fifth *ayllus* of the moieties of Cuzco are represented as the youngest, most subordinate members of their respective moieties. We may therefore conclude, as suggested earlier, that the moiety rankings do indeed appear to build on an integrated age-authority system of classifications similar to that described for the ranking of the ancestral brothers and sisters. The critical distinction between these two instances of age-authority hierarchies is the elaboration of rankings within the moiety system of Cuzco, which comes about by the juxtaposition of the eight *ayllus* within Cuzco with two groups of outsiders; one such group (Sañuq) was composed of people who actually lived outside the city, the other (Uru) was composed of autochthonous, non- and pre-Inkaic peoples. Therefore, from the point of view of the other eight *ayllus* in Cuzco, the fifth *ayllu* of the moieties were "border" groups, that is, distant relatives, or affines. We will return to a more highly contextualized consideration of a similar system of geopolitical classifications later in our discussion of the organization of sociopolitical groups within the District of Pacariqtambo (chapter 4).

In the mythohistorical organization of *ayllus* and moieties in

Cuzco, as it was apparently represented to Sarmiento by his informants, the primordial structures of Inka society were grounded in a complex geopolitical classificatory scheme phrased in terms of a number of complementary oppositions. These included age/authority, male/female, brother/sister, husband/wife, consanguine/affine, and center [Inkas]/periphery [outsiders].

Of the ten *ayllus* that were created at Tampu T'oqo and that later traveled to Cuzco with the Inka ancestors, five appear to have had an especially close relationship with people, places, or ethnic groups within the territory of Pacariqtambo: (1) *Chawin Cuzco Ayllu*, descended from the lineage of Ayar Kachi, who was the third-ranking male ancestor in Sarmiento's version of the origin myth and the first to emerge from Tampu T'oqo in Betanzos's version; (2) *Arayraka Ayllu Cuzco-Kallan*, descended from the lineage of Ayar Uchu, the fourth-ranking male ancestor (Sarmiento) and the second male to emerge from Tampu T'oqo (Betanzos); (3) *Sutiq T'oqo Ayllu*, descended from the window of Sutiq T'oqo at Tampu T'oqo (this is the same window from which the Tambos ethnic group—that is, the group from among which the original ten *ayllus* were formed—emerged at the time of creation); (4) *Maras Ayllu*, descended from the window of Maras T'oqo at Tampu T'oqo (the Maras nation of Indians emerged from this window earlier); and (5) *Maska Ayllu*, identified in historical documents from the early colonial period as members of the Maskas (or Masques) ethnic group. The Maskas Indians lived around Pacariqtambo as well as the present-day communities of Yaurisque, Coyatambo, and Huanoquite (A.D.C., *Archivo del Ilustre Cabildo Justicia y Regimiento del Cuzco*, top. 8, sig. 3−5, 1595, f. 33; see Guaman Poma de Ayala, 1980 [1583−1615]: 84, 337 [339]; Poole, 1984: 91, 458, 464−465).[8]

There is not a great deal more to be said for our purposes here concerning the first two *ayllus* Chawin Cuzco Ayllu and Arayraka Ayllu Cuzco-Kallan. Zuidema has suggested that these two groups were also associated in Inkaic ideology with the pre-Inkaic, autochthonous populations of the valley of Cuzco (1986:23). Ayar Kachi, the founder of Chawin Cuzco Ayllu, maintained a very direct connection with Pacariqtambo in Inka mythohistory; that is, he was walled up inside the cave of Tampu T'oqo soon after the time of creation (see below).

Sutiq T'oqo Ayllu and Maras Ayllu, the two groups in the lower moiety of Cuzco that were descended from the two lateral windows at Tampu T'oqo, appear to have been associated in Inka mythohistory with the capitals of two pre-Inkaic kingdoms located to the north and south of the valley of Cuzco (Zuidema, 1977:274−275,

1986:22–26). Sarmiento says that the Tambos Indians, who lived around Tampu T'oqo, were descended from the window of Sutiq T'oqo. Therefore, by implication, there may have been a close conceptual relationship in Inka ideology between the kindom of Sutiq and the group of Sutiq T'oqo Ayllu within the valley of Cuzco (see Poole, 1984:92). Sutiq is also the name of one of the five traditional ayllus of Paruro, the capital of the province in which the District of Pacariqtambo is located (Poole, 1984).

As the people in the area of Pacariqtambo were identified in colonial historical documents as members of the Maskas ethnic group, it is with Maska Ayllu—the fourth *ayllu* of the lower moiety of Cuzco—that we are most concerned here. In documents dating from the late sixteenth through the mid-nineteenth centuries, the Province of Paruro is referred to as the "province of Chillques and Masques." The Chillkis (Chillques) ethnic group occupied the territory around the town of Paruro (located some 15 kilometers to the east of Pacariqtambo). In late pre-Hispanic and early colonial times, there were also *ayllus* of Chillkis Indians who lived to the west of Cuzco, in the territory of an ethnic confederation known as the Anqu Walloq. The principal ethnic groups included within this confederation were the Pokras, Wankas, and the Chankas (Navarro del Aguila, 1983:87). The Maskas Indians, on the other hand, have traditionally lived within the area approximately coinciding with the modern-day District of Pacariqtambo (see chapter 4).

During Inka times, the Tambos, the Maskas—who may have been an ethnic subgroup of the Tambos (i.e., the people who emerged from the window of Sutiq T'oqo—and the Chillkis were all accorded the status of "Inkas-by-Privilege" (Guaman Poma, 1980 [1583–1615]:750[740]). That is, the political authorities (*kurakas*) of these groups, although themselves not Inka by birth, were accorded the hereditary, privileged status of a provincial seminobility. The Inkas-by-Privilege served as the link between the common *ayllus* and ethnic groups within the circum-Cuzco region and the Inka nobility in Cuzco. The seminoble standing of the Inkas-by-Privilege was determined by, or coincidental with, their affinal status as the husbands of Inka noblewomen. That is, the Inka king gave his "sisters" (both real and classificatory) as wives to these provincial administrators, thus integrating them firmly into the hierarchical, administrative bureaucracy of the empire (Zuidema, 1986:26; see Alberti M., 1985: 570–571; Schaedel, 1978:133).

In summary, *ayllus* were formed among the people who lived around Tampu T'oqo at the time of creation for the purpose of conquering neighboring peoples. The ten *ayllus* were evenly divided into moieties, which were ranked hierarchically. Ranking was also a feature of the relations among the *ayllus* within each moiety. Two of the ten original *ayllus*, Sutiq T'oqo Ayllu and Maska Ayllu, were related to ethnic groups in the area of Pacariqtambo at the time of Spanish contact. These groups—the Tambos and the Maskas—were classified as subordinate affines (i.e., sister's husband) to the Inka nobility in Cuzco.

The origin myth has progressed to this point through the elaboration of kinship relations, phrased in both consanguineal and affinal terms, between the ancestors who emerged from Tampu T'oqo and the privileged *ayllus* (or heads of *ayllus*) and ethnic groups that lived around Pacariqtambo. In the next section, I shall trace the expansion of kinship relations in the myth to include a new generation. In the process, I shall define another level in the mythohistorical connections between Pacariqtambo and Cuzco and we will encounter the clearest expressions of the localization of the origin place of the Inkas.

Notes on the Location of "Pacariqtambo" in Pre-Hispanic Times

After the formation of the ten ayllus at Tampu T'oqo, the ancestors and the *ayllus* set off on their journey to the north in search of fertile land on which to build their capital. As I pointed out earlier, in the versions of the origin myth that were compiled before the time of Sarmiento (i.e., before 1572), there is no indication of precisely where, or even in what direction from Cuzco, "Pacariqtambo" was located. That is, while the origin place is characterized in some early accounts as having been located near Cuzco—for example, Cieza de Leon says that it was "not far from Cuzco" (1967[1553]: 15)—its actual location is not identified in precise directional and topographical terms. This is the case even in what is purportedly the first chronicle written during the colonial period (1542). The document in question (to be discussed in more detail in chapter 3) was composed partially on the basis of testimony provided by four informants, two of whom were said to have been actual natives of Pacariqtambo (Callapiña et al. 1974; Vaca de Castro, 1929).

With Sarmiento's account in 1572, there is a sudden proliferation of toponyms in the area of Pacariqtambo; some of these toponyms can be identified with villages, or sites of old dispersed *ayllus*, located within the area of the modern-day districts of Pacariqtambo and Yaurisque, the latter of which is located between Pacariqtambo and Cuzco. The new toponyms in Sarmiento's account include Waynakancha, Pallata, Tamboquiro, and Haysquisrro. In chronicles writ-

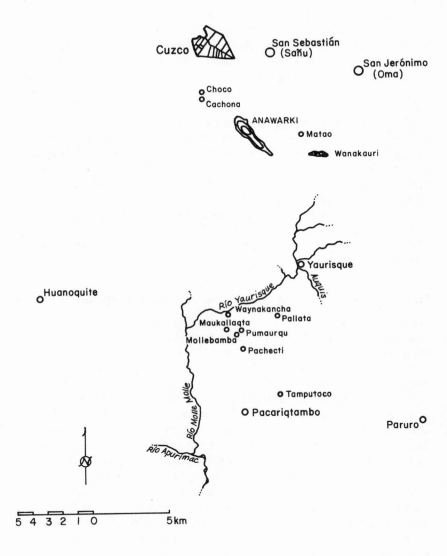

Map 2. The geographical setting of the journey of the ancestors from Pacariqtambo to Cuzco

ten somewhat later than Sarmiento's time, we find one additional toponym, Pachecti (Pachete; Cabello Valboa, 1951[1586]:260–261; Murúa, 1962[1590]:21–22). The locations of the identifiable places are shown on map 2.

Because Sarmiento's version of the origin myth contains these toponyms, we are able to follow the journey of the ancestors from Pacariqtambo to Cuzco in "concrete," geographical space.[9] Although Sarmiento presents us with these unique topographic data, he also presents us most clearly with the problem of the concretization of the cycle of myths concerning the origin of the Inkas from Pacariqtambo. I will first elaborate on this latter problem (to the degree to which it is relevant here) and will then turn to Sarmiento's account of the journey of the ancestors and *ayllus* from Tampu T'oqo to Cuzco.

The Problem of Sarmiento's Concretization of Mythic Space

To put the issue of the concretization of the place of origin in its proper perspective, we should be clear from the beginning about the nature of the "problem" that arises from Sarmiento de Gamboa's version of the origin myth. The problem, or set of problems, may be characterized by the following questions. Given that none of the pre-Sarmiento chronicles identify "Pacariqtambo" with a particular place, was Sarmiento perhaps responsible for distorting what was originally an abstract and dimensionless—or simply a more diffuse—concept of *paqarina* (origin place) when he concretized the origin place of the Inka ancestors and the itinerary of their journey to Cuzco? That is, in his intent to write the *true history* of the Inkas, rather than to assemble a collection of fables, did Sarmiento perhaps prod his informants to get them to identify the origin place in concrete geographical terms? What might Sarmiento's (or his informants') motivations have been for concretizing the place of origin? And finally, is it possible that there existed both an abstract and a concrete conception of "Pacariqtambo" in traditional, pre-Hispanic ideology and mythohistory?

There are two historical circumstances that should be taken into account in evaluating the new character that Sarmiento's account gives to the space of the origin myth. The first concerns the uncertainty that exists with respect to the location of the actual site that was referred to by the name of Pacariqtambo during the period from the mid-1530s through the early 1570s. That is, while there is a town that is named Pacariqtambo today (map 2), *the present-day town did not come into existence until 1571, just one year prior to the completion of Sarmiento's history.* The town of Pacariqtambo

was founded in that year as a *reducción* (reduction) of eleven previously dispersed *ayllus* into a single, nucleated settlement (see
chap. 4). The policy of creating nucleated settlements was instituted
throughout the Andes by Viceroy Francisco de Toledo (1569–1581)
beginning in 1570 and continuing for some five years (Toledo, 1920
[1572–1575]; see also Gade and Escobar, 1982; Málaga M., 1979).
There is, therefore, a curious historical coincidence between the
founding of the town of Pacariqtambo in 1571 and Sarmiento's concretization of the mythic geography of the place of origin in his account of 1572. In light of these observations, the problem for us now
becomes: Was there a place called "Pacariqtambo" before the town
which is known by the name today was founded? I will return to this
question in a moment.

The second historical note that should be taken into account is
that Sarmiento de Gamboa wrote his account of Inka history specifically *for* Francisco de Toledo in order to inform the viceroy of Andean customs, laws, and the nature of the administration of the Inka
empire. The larger purpose to which this information was put was
the assault by Toledo and other officials of the colonial regime
on native authority and autonomy; however, its more immediate
use was in Toledo's reorganization and resettlement of populations
throughout the Andes in the 1570s (see Adorno, 1986: 5; Porras Barrenechea, 1986: 363). Therefore, Sarmiento was both the agent and
the spokesman for the viceroy, who was responsible for the reorganization, and for a new, Spanish-inspired *concretization* of Andean
peoples and places during early colonial times.

Given these circumstances, it is clear that answers to the questions of how and why the place of origin became concretized must
be situated in the context of the historical transformations that
came about in Andean society under Viceroy Toledo. In this light,
the geography of the origin myth, the identities of the ancestors, the
creation of the ten nonroyal *ayllus* at Tampu T'oqo, and other features of the origin myth, as described *to* Sarmiento de Gamboa by
members of the Inka nobility in the early 1570s, take on as much (if
not more) significance as ideological postures and politically motivated historical constructions within the emerging colonial society
than as the basis for a reconstruction of the "true history" of the
Inka empire.

In relation to the two points just raised, we should now consider
in particular the status in early colonial times of four sites identified
in map 2: Maukallaqta, Pumaurqu, Pacariqtambo, and Tamputoco. I
will argue here that these four sites can be divided into two pairs.

Maukallaqta and Pumaurqu represent the probable sites of "Pacariqtambo" and "Tampu T'oqo" *before* the founding of the "new" town (i.e., the *reducción*) of Pacariqtambo in 1571. The places known today as Pacariqtambo and Tamputoco appear to have received these names—and come to be associated with the origin places of the Inkas—sometime *after* 1571. I will clarify certain points concerning this hypothesis here; however, my main discussion of the founding of the present-day town of Pacariqtambo, and the significance of this process for the reorganization of local *ayllus* in and around both the old *and* the new Pacariqtambo, must await a more thorough discussion of the *ayllu* organization within the region of the District of Pacariqtambo in early colonial times (see chap. 4).

In map 2, there is a place called *Tamputoco* located some 2 to 3 kilometers to the northeast of the town of Pacariqtambo. Tamputoco is a limestone outcrop that has one small cave and several smaller cavities in the rock face (plate 1). People in the town of Pacariqtambo today say that the cave in the rock outcrop of Tamputoco is the place of emergence of the Inka ancestors. (This toponym appears on the 1:100,000 map of Cuzco published by the Peruvian Instituto Geográfico Militar, 1981.)

However, the rock outcrop called Tamputoco is not the only site in the region identified by people today as the Tampu T'oqo of the origin myth. Six kilometers to the north of the town of Pacariqtambo, near the incorporated community of Mollebamba—Ayllo Pachecti, there are two archaeological sites, called Maukallaqta (ancient town) and Pumaurqu (puma mountain). The large and well-preserved ruins of the town of Maukallaqta have been surveyed and described by a number of archaeologists, including Bauer (*n.d.*), Bingham (1930), Muelle (1950), and Pardo (1946, 1957). In a study of archaeological sites in the Province of Paruro carried out from 1984 to 1987, Bauer thoroughly mapped the ruins of Maukallaqta and excavated at some four locations within the site (*n.d.*). He concluded that Maukallaqta was occupied from the Middle Horizon period (ca. A.D. 500—1100) until the time of the Spanish conquest (plate 2).

A short distance to the east of Maukallaqta lies the small but prominent rock outcrop called Pumaurqu. There are ruins of a number of small buildings around the base of Pumaurqu, as well as two finely carved pumas and other elaborate stone carvings on top of the rock outcrop (plate 3). In addition, there are several small caves in the northern cliff face overlooking the buildings at the base of the outcrop. Pumaurqu is considered to be the site of Tampu T'oqo by people in the town of Mollebamba—Ayllo Pachecti and the surround-

Plate 1. Tamputoco

ing area. At least two archaeologists who have conducted research in the region also claim this status for the site of Pumaurqu (Bauer, *n.d.;* Pardo, 1946).

In a document included in the petition submitted in 1964 by the neighboring settlements of Mollebamba and Ayllo Pachecti for recognition as an incorporated "peasant community" (*comunidad campesina*), there is a reference dating to 1643 to a place referred to as "el pueblo viejo de Pacarictambo" (the old town of Pacarictambo). The document states that this site was located on a mountain called Viracocha-urqu (A.M.A.C., exp. #4281). As I will show later, this reference almost certainly identifies the ruins of Maukallaqta as the

Plate 2. Maukallaqta and environs: *a*, Maukallaqta; *b*, Pumaurqu; *c*, Mollebamba

Plate 3. Pumaurqu (Tampu T'oqo). Photo by Brian Bauer

Plate 4. Mollebamba–Ayllo Pachecti and vicinity: *a,* Maukallaqta; *b,* Mollebamba; *c,* Ayllo Pachecti; *d,* Pacariqtambo

original site of Pacariqtambo—that is, before 1571—at least, accord-ing to the interpretation of people in the area of Mollebamba and Ayllo Pachecti during the early seventeenth century.

Because of the elaborate Inka constructions at Maukallaqta and Pumaurqu, and because of the documentary evidence mentioned above, it seems reasonable to identify the former site with the Paca-riqtambo of Inka times and the latter site with the cave of origin, Tampu T'oqo. However, this conclusion should be taken as provi-sional, for it masks a number of complications (which I will only hint at here) concerning conflicts in the appropriation of the "his-tory" of the origin place of the Inkas by different groups within the district of Pacariqtambo today as well as differences of opinion among these groups with respect to the location of places associated with the origin.

To summarize briefly some of the problems just alluded to, the name "Pacariqtambo," which (as pointed out earlier) may originally have identified the ruins of Maukallaqta near the community of Mollebamba–Ayllo Pachecti (plate 4), appears to have been transferred from the ruins of Maukallaqta southward to the present-day town sometime during the period from the 1570s to the 1590s (i.e., after the building of the *reducción* of Pacariqtambo in 1571). As a result of this translation, or translocation, of the name of the *town* of origin, the actual *cave* of origin, Tampu T'oqo, may have shifted southward as well, coming to rest at the small cave northeast of the town of Pacariqtambo and identified today by the name Tamputoco. A possible motivation for the change in the locations of the places associated with the origin of the Inkas may have been an attempt by people in the town of Pacariqtambo (which is the capital of the modern-day district of the same name) to appropriate the prestige of the origin place of the Inkas from the small community of Mollebamba–Ayllo Pachecti.

Until I can discuss these problems more thoroughly (in chap. 4), the references to Tampu T'oqo in the following discussion should be taken to indicate the site located to the north of Pacariqtambo, near Mollebamba and Ayllo Pachecti, which is known today as Pumaurqu.

The Journey of the Ancestors from Pacariqtambo to Cuzco

In Sarmiento's account of the origin myth, he says that the Inkas set out on their legendary journey from Tampu T'oqo under the direction of their determined leaders, Mama Waku and Manqo Qhapaq. Cabello Valboa (1951 [1568]:261) and Murúa (1962 [1590]:21–23) say that the Inkas first stopped at Pachecti, located 5 kilometers north of the town of Pacariqtambo (see map 2, Ayllo Pachecti). At Pachecti, they tested the soil and, finding it unsuitable, they moved on. The next stop—the first in Sarmiento's account—was at Waynakancha, which was said to be located "four leagues [ca. 22 kilometers] from Cuzco." It is important to note that there is a small Inka-period site called Waynakancha located in the Yaurisque Valley, near the Hacienda Waynakancha (Bauer, n.d.; map 2).

At Waynakancha, Manqo Qhapaq and his sister Mama Oqllu conceived a child. The entourage then moved on to a place called "Tamboquiro" (unidentified), where Mama Oqllu gave birth to a boy whom they named Sinchi Ruq'a. Sinchi Ruq'a would grow up to succeed his father as the second king of the empire. After celebrating the birth of Sinchi Ruq'a, the ancestors moved on to Pallata (Palluta), "which is virtually the same place as Tamboquiro." The entourage remained in Pallata for several years. However, as they were not satisfied with the land there, they moved on to "Haysquisrro," which was said to be located one-quarter league from Pallata (Sarmiento, 1942 [1572]: 51–52). The toponym "Haysquisrro" may be a corruption of the name Yaurisque, a town to the northeast of Pallata, or perhaps it refers to a place in the nearby Auquis River Valley (map 2). We should note here that the chronicler Ramos Gavilán states that Pacariqtambo was located "7 or 8 leagues [38.5–40 kilometers] from Cuzco, toward *Taurisca*" (1976 [1621]: 14; my emphasis). The name "Taurisca" almost certainly refers to the town known today as Yaurisque.

It was at Haysquisrro that the event occurred that simultaneously broke the unity among the ancestors and established a permanent connection between the ancestors and Tampu T'oqo. One of the four brothers, Ayar Kachi, was a great trickster; he was cruel and very handy with a sling. Ayar Kachi made trouble in all of the villages through which the entourage passed, and he disturbed the peace and harmony among the ancestors. Therefore, the other seven ancestors conspired to get rid of him by a ruse. They sent Ayar Kachi back to retrieve some items that they said they had left in the cave of Tampu T'oqo. The ancestors sent along with Ayar Kachi a person from their entourage named Tambochakay (*tambo* entrance-barrer). The latter was instructed to kill Ayar Kachi. Arriving at Tampu T'oqo, Ayar Kachi went inside the cave, whereupon Tambochakay immediately shoved a large boulder across the entrance, trapping Ayar Kachi inside, where he remained for all time (Sarmiento, 1942 [1572]: 52–54).

Having rid themselves of Ayar Kachi, the ancestors moved on and arrived next in the immediate environs of the valley of Cuzco at a place called Quirirmanta, at the foot of a mountain called Wanakauri. Ascending Wanakauri, the ancestors viewed for the first time the valley of Cuzco (map 2). Recognizing by the sign of a rainbow that stretched over the valley that this was their long-sought-after home, the ancestors prepared to descend into the valley. At this point, Ayar Uchu (the fourth ancestor brother) was transformed into stone; the Inkas later worshiped this stone as one of their principal sacred sites (*wakas*). The remaining six ancestors went from Wanakauri to a place called "Matawa" (Matao?; map 2), where they remained for two years. They then entered Cuzco, and when they arrived at the place that would become the center of the city, Wanaypata, Ayar Awka (the second male ancestor) was transformed into a stone pillar. This left Manqo Qhapaq, his four sisters, and the boy Sinchi Ruq'a to found and build the city of Cuzco (Sarmiento, 1942 [1572]: 54–57).

We will leave the origin myth at this point, as the outline establishes the principal events that occurred during the legendary journey from Pacariqtambo to Cuzco and identifies several toponyms along the route of that journey as recorded by Sarmiento de Gamboa, Cabello Valboa, and Murúa. Before turning to a more detailed consideration of the concretization of the place of origin and the historicizing of this cycle of myths in the Spanish chronicles, we must pause for a moment to consider what the mythohistorical account summarized here is about. In this, we cannot be exhaustive, and I will not pretend that these comments will shed light on the profound symbolism lying just beneath the surface of this rich mythohistorical tradition (e.g., in the etymologies of the names of the ancestors and the ten *ayllus*; in the heroic personalities and deeds of the ancestors, and so on). Analyses of these and other related aspects of the symbolism of the origin myth have been undertaken elsewhere by other authors (e.g., Rostworowski, 1983; Urbano, 1981, 1987; Zuidema, 1973, 1986).

What should be emphasized for our interpretation of the origin myth here are the following points. As is undoubtedly true of all origin myths, the Inka origin myth is concerned essentially with the sources, nature, and consequences of *identity*. These concerns are seen on three levels in the Inka origin myth: individual, social, and political. The first—*individual* identity—has its clearest expressions in the personalities of the ancestors. These are eight characters, each with his or her distinctive personality, "function," and life history. The ancestors were a group of carefully constructed archetypes, for example, the king, the queen, the tyrant, and the trickster, whose individual and collective identities were the refraction through the lens of Inka mythohistory of the array of personalities of which each generation of storytellers found itself a part.

The concern with *social* identity in the origin myth is seen in the relations ascribed to the ancestral men and women (e.g., the siblings and/or spouses) and in the formation of nonroyal *ayllus* among the commoners as one of the first acts undertaken by the ancestors. The origin myth is explicit about the sources of social identity for both the Inka nobility and the commoners. The Inkas who emerged from Tampu T'oqo at the command of T'iqsi Wiraqocha were of divine origin, and their social identities—the first principles of Inka collective life—were products of their divinely inspired *individual* identities. The social identities of the commoners, on the other hand, were derived from, and dependent on, the Inkas, for it was the ancestors who were responsible for the formation of the first *ayllus*. Thus, as it was apparently represented to Sarmiento by his (noble) informants, the origin myth describes a hierarchy of identities. T'iqsi Wiraqocha → Inka nobility → commoner *ayllus*. The chief consequence of this hierarchy of sources of identity was to provide a rationale for the inequalities of status and class that existed in the empire.

The final point concerns the question of *where* these definitions of identity took place. The myth situates these processes outside Cuzco, but within its immediate environs. In a sense, the concern here is with the problem of establishing a point of view within mythic space from which to characterize the array of *political* identities within the empire, especially the relationship between the nobility in Cuzco and the Inkas-by-Privilege and local *kurakas* in the provinces. For this, neither the center nor the extremities of the empire would do, since Cuzco and populations on the periphery of the empire were far removed from each other in both geography and history. The compromise was to select a middle place, that is, a "boundary" place with one side on the periphery of the valley of Cuzco and another adjacent to what was geographically and historically "outside." Pacariqtambo was not the only place on the border of Cuzco that met these criteria, but it was, for reasons that we can only hint at here, the place that was selected (at least in many of the accounts recorded during early colonial times) for this purpose. Once set in motion on the periphery, the personalities, structures, and relations governing imperial society (e.g., the ancestors, *ayllus*, moieties, and hierarchical ranking) moved inexorably toward the center, defining successive boundaries between the periphery and the center in the journey of the ancestors, until they came to rest in the valley of Cuzco.

With the overview of the Inka origin myth presented in this chapter as a background, we will examine two central issues in the remainder of this study: first, the roles of Sarmiento de Gamboa and certain of his informants in concretizing and historicizing "Pacariqtambo" in imperial mythohistory; and second, the surprising success that certain elite individuals in Pacariqtambo had during early colonial times in orchestrating the mythohistory of the origin of the empire into local genealogical history.

3. The Role of the Urban and Provincial Elite in Historicizing Inka Mythohistory

A Note on Nobility and Privilege in Early Colonial Peru

The documents discussed in this chapter concern claims to noble status that were made in connection with the myth of origin by a number of individuals during the early colonial period. Therefore, it is useful to establish from the outset the bases on which such claims were made and what the consequences were for individuals and families whose claims were recognized by the Spanish.

One of the principal aims of the reorganization of the colonial administrative bureaucracy carried out by Viceroy Toledo during the early 1570s was to establish an efficient system for the assessment and collection of tribute. The unit for such assessment was the *repartimiento*, an administrative unit based on the nonterritorial grant to a Spaniard of patronage over a group of Indians. The Indians within each *repartimiento* were grouped into one or more nucleated towns; these were the reductions (*reducciones*). Each *repartimiento* was assessed a fixed sum of tribute to be paid in specie and products on a biannual basis; each taxpayer was assigned a share of the total tax levy (see Toledo, 1975 [1583]).

The amount of tribute levied against each *repartimiento* was determined on the basis of a census of the eligible taxpayers. The censuses, which were first carried out in a massive campaign of "inspections" (*visitas*) undertaken by Spanish officials in the early 1570s (a process that was coordinated with the institution of the reductions) ideally identified all adults and children in each community by name, age, and sex. The class of taxpayers included men between the ages of eighteen and fifty years old. Women, children, and the disabled were exempt from paying taxes (Toledo, 1867 [1573]: 187–189; Villarán, 1964: 93). Community officials—called *caciques* or *kurakas*—were also exempt from taxes. Among their duties was the collection of the taxes (Toledo, 1867 [1573]: 186). In the system of local governance instituted by Toledo, the principal local officials, all of whom were regularly exempt from paying taxes, included a governor, a *cacique principal,* two *caciques* (also called *segundas personas*), and officials, variously referred to as *cacique, segunda,* and *mandón,* who represented the *ayllus* (Glave, 1987:81; Hampe, 1986:184; Villarán, 1964:93). In addition, individuals who could demonstrate that they had belonged to the Inka nobility in pre-Hispanic times were exempt from paying taxes and from performing public labor and personal service for the Spaniards (Hampe, 1986: 184; Rowe, 1957:156–157; Spalding, 1984:219–221; Toledo, 1867 [1573]:186).

Each claim to noble status had to be argued before the Spanish authorities and supported with documentation, generally in the form of corroborating testimony supplied by recognized members of the Inka nobility. As there were considerable advantages to be gained from being accorded noble status, a large number of such claims were made. The historical documents from Pacariqtambo and the surrounding area (especially Yaurisque and Paruro) suggest that individuals or families who might actually have had the status of Inkas-by-Privilege, that is, *semi*-nobles, under the Inkas may have used such status for claiming *noble* descent in colonial times (see Poole, 1984:95). That such may have been the case in the area of Pacariq-tambo is suggested by what at least one Spanish official in 1791 took to be an unusually large number of dubious claims to noble descent coming from this area. This observation is contained in a letter from the official in charge of taxation (the *fiscal superior*) in Paruro to the head of the *doctrina* (ecclesiastical district) of Yaurisque (Pacariq-tambo was within the *doctrina* of Yaurisque): "in the doctrina of Yaurisque of this district [Paruro] there exist a considerable number of Indians who claim to be nobles and who, lacking documents proving their noble lineage, have given oral testimony to justify the truth of their allegation" (A.D.C., *Intendencia, Real Hacienda*).[1] The *fiscal superior* went on to state that unless people could back up their claims to noble status with documentation, they were to be classified as tribute payers.

In Pacariqtambo, as elsewhere in the Andes, there appears to have been a certain degree of continuity in the families from which the *caciques principales* were drawn in early colonial times and those individuals who were recognized as descendants of Inka nobility (see Rowe, 1957:157). One example of this is seen in the appearance of the members of a certain family, the Callapiñas, as governors and *caciques principales* in Pacariqtambo and Yaurisque from the middle of the sixteenth century through the eighteenth century. In 1568, for example, the *cacique principal,* "the lord of all the *repartimiento* of Pacariqtambo," was a man named Pedro Calla Piña (Callapiña). The Callapiñas were a powerful family in the local bureaucracies in Pacariqtambo and Yaurisque, and, as we will see later, they appear to have played a central role in historicizing the Inka origin myth through their claims to noble descent.

The foregoing discussion provides a context for the examination of a number of claims to noble ancestry that were made by people from Pacariqtambo. Before examining a series of claims made by the Callapiña family beginning in 1569, we will make a brief detour through another document that testifies to the role of what was probably a member of this same family in recounting the earliest "official" version of the Inka origin myth. This occurred in 1542, only one decade after the Spanish conquest of Peru.

The Chronicle of the *Khipukamayuqs*

In 1892, Jiménez de la Espada published a document under the title *Una antigüalla peruana,* "A Peruvian Relic" (see Duviols, 1979a, and Porras Barrenechea, 1986, for histories of the redaction of this document). Although the document, which I will refer to here as the Chronicle of the *Khipukamayuqs,* is signed at the end by a "Fray Antonio," whose further identity is unknown, and dated Cuzco, 1608, the chronicle is attributed the date of 1542 in two later editions (Vaca de Castro, 1929 [1542/1608]; Callapiña et al., 1974 [1542/1608]). The reason for the attribution of this earlier date is that near the beginning of the narrative, it is stated that the document is the record of an inquest held by Licenciado Vaca de Castro in Cuzco in 1542. The purpose of this inquest was to ascertain the true history of the Inka empire.

Vaca de Castro's informants at the inquest were four old *khipukamayuqs* who had served the Inkas as official historians before the conquest. Two of these men identified themselves as natives of Pacariqtambo; their names were Callapiña and Supno (Callapiña et al., 1974 [1542/1608]: 24). In their testimony, these two men claimed authority in matters having to do with the history of the Inkas on the grounds that not only they, but Manqo Qhapaq (the first Inka king) and *his* ancestors as well, were from Pacariqtambo. "These [two informants, Callapiña and Supno] stated that their parents and grandparents, as they were *quipucamayos* of the Incas, told their children and grandchildren—committing them to silence on the matter—that the first Inca Manco Capac was the son of a lord *curaca* of Pacariqtambo, whose name they did not know" (Callapiña et al., 1974 [1542/1608]: 24–25). I will return to consider the role of the two *khipukamayuqs* from Pacariqtambo in the early history of the concretization and historicizing of the Inka origin myth after explaining the nature of the document in which their testimony is recorded.

As both Duviols (1979*a*) and Porras Barrenechea (1986) have pointed out, the Chronicle of the *Khipukamayuqs* is clearly divisible into two parts. The first recounts the "history" of the Inka kings from Manqo Qhapaq through Pachakuti Inka and gives descriptions of Inka political, social, and religious institutions and customs. The second part of the chronicle describes the life and deeds of Wayna Qhapaq, the last (eleventh) Inka king, who died just before the arrival of the Spaniards. The narrative describes the struggle for power and succession to the throne between Atawallpa and Waskar, two of Wayna Qhapaq's sons. Atawallpa and Waskar both died during the year following the conquest, and a dispute raged throughout the next few decades concerning which of several possible lines of descent the Spanish should recognize as the legitimate heirs to the royal title. The Chronicle of the *Khipukamayuqs* is not impartial on this question. However, in order to follow the argument that is made in the chronicle with respect to this issue, it is necessary first to discuss briefly the origin myths that appear in the first part of the chronicle.

The Chronicle of the *Khipukamayuqs* actually contains two versions of the origin of the Inka Manqo Qhapaq. The first is a general account, which apparently was related by all four of Vaca de Castro's informants. In this version, it is stated that Manqo Qhapaq, who is said to have been engendered by the rays of the sun, emerged from a window in a house of Caparitambo [*sic*], which was located five leagues (ca. 28 kilometers) from Cuzco. Manqo Qhapaq then left for the valley of Cuzco, taking with him two old priests, ten or twelve Indians with their wives, and an idol called Wanakauri (Callapiña et al., 1974: 23–24).

The second version of the origin myth, which is attributed specifically to the two *khipukamayuqs* from Pacariqtambo, Callapiña and Supno, states that Manqo Qhapaq was the son of a *kuraka* (*cacique principal*) of Pacariqtambo. The boy grew up alone with his father, his mother having died when he was a baby. In a spirit of playfulness, Manqo Qhapaq's father called him by the nickname, "Son of the Sun." When Manqo Qhapaq was ten or twelve years old, his father died. The boy, as well as the "stupid people" (*gente bruta*) of the town, were left with the notion that he was the Son of the Sun. Now, in Manqo Qhapaq's family there were two old men who were the priests of the idols of Manqo Qhapaq's father. These men continued to promote the "hoax" (*patraña*) that Manqo was a divine being. When Manqo Qhapaq reached the age of eighteen or twenty, the two old priests convinced him that he was indeed the Son of the Sun and they encouraged him in the belief that he and his descendants were the natural lords of the earth. Animated by these pretensions, Manqo Qhapaq set out from Pacariqtambo with his family, the two priests, and the idol called Wanakauri to claim his rightful place as lord of the valley of Cuzco (Callapiña et al., 1974 [1542/1608]: 24–29; for a similar view of the origin myth as a hoax perpetrated on the people by Manqo Qhapaq, see Ramos Gavilán, 1976 [1621]: 14–15).

As Duviols has shown (1979a), the overall thrust of the Chronicle of the *Khipukamayuqs* concerns a claim to the Inka title that was brought at the beginning of the seventeenth century by a man named don Melchor Carlos Inka. Don Melchor was the grandson of a man named Paullu Inka. Paullu was a son of Wayna Qhapaq by a secondary wife, a high-ranking princess who belonged to the provincial nobility. The descendants of Paullu Inka were among those who were contending for succession to the Inka throne after the death of Atawallpa and Waskar.

It was in the context of this dispute that don Melchor Carlos Inka made his claim to the throne by means of what was a decidedly novel argument. That is, don Melchor claimed that Inka rule was essentially illegitimate, given the fact that the dynasty founded by Manqo Qhapaq had gained power by means of a ruse perpetrated on the people. Therefore, those who were in a direct line of descent from the Inkas—such as Waskar and his descendants—were likewise illegitimate rulers. This argument, pointing to the "global illegitimacy" of Inka rule, cleared the way for don Melchor Carlos Inka's somewhat paradoxical claim to the throne. He argued that, while he was not in a *direct* line of descent from these illegitimate rulers, but as he was of *more* noble pedigree than such pretenders to the throne as Atawallpa and his successors, he (don Melchor) should be recognized as the legitimate heir to the throne (Duviols, 1979a: 586–587).

In its overall thrust, then, the Chronicle of the *Khipukamayuqs* is nothing more than an elaborately constructed claim to the Inka title that was brought before the Spanish by don Melchor Carlos Inka. This is not to say, however, that the material provided in the testimony of the four *khipukamayuqs* is fraudulent. Rather, the information contained in the sections of the chronicle reporting their testimony probably did come from extracts recorded at the inquest held by Vaca de Castro in 1542 (Duviols, 1979a: 588–589; Porras Barrenechea, 1986: 748). With their references to the *khipukamayuqs* from Pacariqtambo and the detailed information they provide on the Inka dynasty and Inka customs, the 1542 extracts were used by don Melchor—or, more likely, by his scribe—to enhance the credibility of his claim to the Inka throne.

The material from the 1542 extracts in the Chronicle of the *Khipukamayuqs* does not identify the precise location of the origin place, Pacariqtambo. In fact, there is very little local (Pacariqtambo) knowledge contained in the testimony from the 1542 extracts. The only point on which I think one can perhaps see an element of local, technical knowledge is in the reference to "*chotas*," a term that is used in the document to refer to stretches, or lengths of measurement, along the Inka roads (Callapiña et al., 1974 [1542/1608]: 37). The word *chota* is not common in historical or ethnographic materials outside of Pacariqtambo. In fact, apart from references to this word in dictionaries from colonial to contemporary times, *chota* (or *chuta*) is explicitly mentioned elsewhere only in Francisco de Avila's account of myths and rituals in the central Andean town of Huarochirí (Avila, 1966 [1608]: 142–145; see also Zuidema's discussions of the word *chapa* as a possible synonym for *chuta*, 1986: 30, and *n.d.*). On the other hand, there is a very rich body of lore and social practice connected with the word *chota* (*chuta*, *chhiuta*) in the area of Pacariqtambo today (See Urton, 1984, 1988, and *n.d.a*). Therefore, the word may have been (as it still may be) a local technical term whose use by the *khipukamayuqs* in 1542 lends some credence to their claim of having been natives of Pacariqtambo.

While the Chronicle of the *Khipukamayuqs* does not directly concretize the space of the place of origin, it does introduce into the written record the name of Pacariqtambo as the place from where Manqo Qhapaq originated, and it identifies the first Inka as a member of a lineage of *caciques principales* there. In addition, the testimony in the Chronicle of the *Khipukamayuqs* establishes the fact that in 1542, a member of the Callapiña family from Pacariqtambo was recognized as an authority on the history of the supposed events surrounding Manqo Qhapaq's ascension to power. In the next section, we will follow the argument made in 1569 by a *cacique principal* from Pacariqtambo named Callapiña who *himself* claimed to be a direct descendant of the first Inka king, Manqo Qhapaq.

The Descendants of Manqo Qhapaq and Qoya Qori Kuka

The focus of the discussion in this section concerns claims to the status of Inka nobility that were brought before the Spanish in Cuzco by members of the Callapiña family in 1569, 1692, and 1718. In the earliest of these proceedings, a man from Pacariqtambo named Rodrigo Sutiq Callapiña claimed to be a direct descendant of Manqo Qhapaq on his father's patriline and of other Inka nobility on his mother's patriline. We do not know what relationship, if any, may have existed between Rodrigo Sutiq Callapiña and the *khipukamayuq* from Pacariqtambo named Callapiña who testified before Vaca de Castro in Cuzco in 1542.

A word should be said at the beginning concerning the nature of the documentation used in this discussion. The principal document to be used here, what I will refer to as the Callapiña Document, is one of several original documents at present in the private collection of the Coronel family, the owners of an hacienda in Pacariqtambo.[2] For various reasons, which we need not go in to here, it is fairly certain that the documents in question have been in private hands at least since the 1930s. Copies of some of the documents in this collection (although not the Callapiña Document itself) were used in the preparation of the petition for the official recognition of the community of Pacariqtambo as a *comunidad de indígenas* (native community) in 1944 (A.M.A.C., exp. #5877). As the Callapiña Document is of such great interest and importance to Andean ethnohistory, a transcription appears in the Appendix.

The bulk of the material in the Callapiña Document concerns testimony that was given in Cuzco in 1569 in support of a claim to noble status made by Rodrigo Sutiq Callapiña, a native of Pacariqtambo. The material from this earlier inquest was copied in connection with similar proceedings carried out in 1692 and 1718. In 1692, Rodrigo's two grandsons, Juan Santa Cruz hanco sutiq Callapiña and Thomas hanco sutiq Callapiña, petitioned for noble status and had a copy of the testimony from their grandfather's inquest entered as the principal evidence supporting their own claim. The material from 1569 was copied again in 1718 as the basis for the reaffirmation of the noble status of the Callapiña lineage by Rodrigo's great-grandsons, Vicente and Ysidro Callapiña. Vicente and Ysidro lived in Yaurisque. Therefore, the Callapiña Document, which appears in the Appendix, is a copy made in 1718 of a 1692 copy of the original petition for noble status made in 1569.[3] A diagram of the genealogical relationships described in the Callapiña Document is given in figure 1.

In 1569, Rodrigo Sutiq Callapiña successfully argued that he was a direct patrilineal descendant of Manqo Qhapaq, "the first king of this land." On his maternal side, he claimed that his mother, Angelina Qori Qoyllur (Coricoyllor), was the granddaughter of two members of the Inka nobility, Kilaku Yupanki Inka (Quilaco Yupanqui Ynga) and Qoya Qori Kuka (Coya Coricoca). Rodrigo Sutiq Calla-

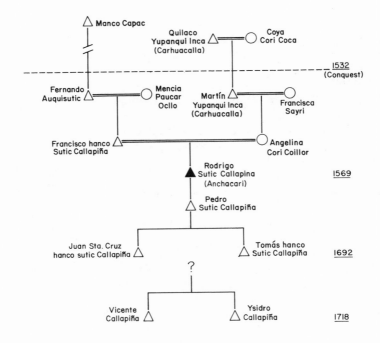

Fig. 1. The genealogy of Rodrigo Sutiq Callapiña

piña called on eight witnesses to testify in his behalf. The witnesses, men ranging in age (they claimed) from 85 to 132 years, were recognized descendants of the Inka nobility in Cuzco.[4] As we will see later, at least one of the witnesses—and very probably two others as well—was a principal informant for Sarmiento de Gamboa's *Historia de los Incas*.

The Origin Myth in the Construction of Local Genealogical History

The Callapiña Document is a remarkably rich source of information for constructing the genealogical history of a local lineage of *caciques principales* in Pacariqtambo and Yaurisque from the mid-sixteenth to the early eighteenth centuries, as well as for understanding the connections between elite families in Cuzco and Pacariqtambo during the late sixteenth century. It is in the context of these connections that we must place the sixteenth-century constructions of the mythohistorical tradition of the origin of Manqo Qhapaq from Pacariqtambo. It is particularly important in this regard to note that the Callapiña Document contains two "new" versions of the Inka origin myth. These versions concretize and historicize the Inka origin place not only in geographical terms, but also in terms of local genealogical history. That is, Manqo Qhapaq is identified (by inference) as the ancestor of a lineage of a particular *ayllu* in Pacariqtambo: Anchacari (Aqchakar) Ayllu.

We will turn first to the two origin myths recorded in the 1569 extracts in the Callapiña Document. After presenting these mytho-historical accounts, we will consider two problems that emerge from them: first, the place of Manqo Qhapaq and his presumed lineal descendants in the organization of *ayllus* and moieties in Pacariqtambo; and second, the possible role of Rodrigo Sutiq Callapiña's great-grandmother, Qoya Qori Kuka (Queen Golden Coca), and her matrilineage in the mythohistorical and geopolitical relations between Pacariqtambo and Cuzco in pre-Hispanic times.

To the best of my knowledge, the two versions of the Inka origin myth translated below are the only accounts—purportedly given by indigenous testimony—that have become available to us *after* the versions that were recorded in the early seventeenth-century chronicles of Santacruz Pachacuti Yamqui (1613) and Guaman Poma de Ayala (1583–1615). The first account is contained in the joint testimony given in 1569 by Diego Atao Yupanqui ("85 years old") and Santiago Aucamira ("93 years old"). Both of these men were said to be *yngas naturales* (native Inkas, i.e., nobility) of Cuzco. The account reads as follows:

> [These two witnesses] had heard the ancient tradition from their elders and the more ancient ones how the said *Ynga Manco Capac was born from a window that they call Tambo Toco,* which is in a rock outcrop three leagues from this city [of Cuzco] in the valley of Tambo and near to this rock outcrop is another rock outcrop and in that one *there is another window, which they call Marastoco.* And they [the two witnesses] also know that the said don Rodrigo Sutic Callapiña and his parents and grandparents since the time of the Inca have all been and are considered as Inca nobility and descendants of the said Manco Capac Ynga. As such they never paid tribute nor served in *tambos* [way stations along the Inca roads] nor did *mitas* [turns of public labor] nor personal service before they were governors of their town. (See Appendix, p. 132; my emphasis)

The second version of the origin myth is included in the joint testimony provided by Martín Natipi Yupanqui ("132 years old") and Francisco Apuranti ("108 years old"). These two men, who actually lived in the town of Larapac in the *encomienda* of Pedro Alonso Carrasco, identified themselves as *compadres* (ritual coparents) of Rodrigo Sutiq Callapiña (see Appendix, p. 137). Their account is translated below:

> They [the two witnesses] say they know don Rodrigo Sutic Callapiña *Casique principal* and governor of *Ayllo Anchacari* reduced in the town of Pacariqtambo . . . they also know don Martín Yupanqui maternal grandfather of the said don Rodrigo Sutic Callapiña and they are aware of the ancient tradition of the native lord *Ynga manco capac* who was of this land and who *was born from a window* that is in a rock outcrop in the town of Pacariqtambo three leagues from this city *which they call Tamputoco* and *near this is another window called marastoco* and that in the time of *Guascar Ynga* they knew Quilaco Yupanqui Ynga of *Ayllo Caruacalla* of the said town and the Coya Coricoca great-grandparents of the said don Rodrigo Sutic Callapiña who died "*gentiles*" [i.e., without being baptized] before the Spaniards came to this kingdom. (Appendix, p. 137; my emphasis)

There are several points of interest in these two accounts. Both state that Manqo Qhapaq came from the window of Tampu T'oqo in Pacariqtambo. The accounts also mention Maras T'oqo, which, in Sarmiento's version of the origin myth, was the window of origin of both the Maras Indians and Maras Ayllu. However, these two accounts say nothing about the third window, which is generally included in the origin myth, Sutiq T'oqo. This was the window from which emerged Sutiq T'oqo Ayllu and the Tambos Indians. It will be recalled that the Tambos Indians composed the major ethnic group in the area of Pacariqtambo.

Concerning the absence of an explicit reference to Sutiq T'oqo, it is no doubt significant that the man in whose behalf these testimonies were given was named Rodrigo *Sutiq* (Sutic) Callapiña. Rodrigo's father and grandfather also bore the surname Sutiq, a Quechua word that means "of the name." It may have been the case that the mention of the surname Sutiq was tantamount to a reference to the window of Sutiq T'oqo, for there seems to have been a connection of *sutiq* as a surname, a toponym, and an *ayllu* name at this time. For instance, one of the two headmen of Sutiq T'oqo Ayllu in Cuzco in

1572 was named don Francisco Auca Micho Auri Sutic (Sarmiento, 1942 [1572]: 50).

If the foregoing inference were the case, then it seems that the informants from Cuzco in 1569 may have considered Rodrigo Sutiq Callapiña's lineage to have descended not only from Tampu T'oqo (via Manqo Qhapaq) but also from Sutiq T'oqo (via the ethnic affiliation of this lineage with the Tambos Indians). The agency for this double descent would appear to have been Rodrigo's *ayllu* affiliation. That is, Rodrigo Sutiq Callapiña is identified in the document as a high-ranking member of *ayllu* Anchacari (also written in the document as "Anchaca"). We will see later that an *ayllu* of this name (i.e., Aqchakar) belonged to the upper moiety of Pacariqtambo in the 1560s.

We should note that, according to Inka inheritance practices, men inherited their *ayllu* affiliation through their patriline, women through their matriline (Zuidema, 1977: 255–256). As Rodrigo claimed patrilineal descent from Manqo Qhapaq, the implication is that Manqo Qhapaq, who emerged from Tampu T'oqo, was the founder-ancestor of Anchacari *ayllu* in Pacariqtambo. On the other hand, one of the principal families of Anchacari *ayllu* during the sixteenth century appears to have been the Sutiq lineage. In a document from 1568 (to be discussed later), the headman of Anchacari (Anchaca, Acchacara) *ayllu* was named Luis Sutiq.

Thus, Rodrigo Sutiq Callapiña combined in his ancestry descent from both Tampu T'oqo and Sutiq T'oqo; the former established his link—probably as a member of the Inka-by-Privilege class—to the Inka nobility in Cuzco; the latter indicated his affiliation with an *ayllu* of the Maskas, a subgroup of the Tambos ethnic group, which inhabited the Pacariqtambo area.

When seen in terms of the claims made by Rodrigo Sutiq Callapiña for his paternal ancestry, it seems clear from the testimony in 1569 that the Inka origin myth was being manipulated within a network of high-status individuals in Cuzco and Pacariqtambo partially to take advantage of certain features of the Spanish colonial administrative system. That is, these members of the provincial and urban elite were calling up for the Spanish officials names and places of the origin myth as a part of a strategy for maneuvering a certain lineage of Inkas-by-Privilege into a position of advantage within the new political landscape that was taking shape with the reforms initiated by Viceroy Toledo. Except in the case of the two witnesses who were Rodrigo's *compadres* (Martín Natipi Yupanqui and Francisco Apuranti), it is not immediately apparent what the motives of the witnesses—all of whom were Inka noblemen—were for participating in this legal proceeding. We will take up this question later as it is a central issue in the history of the concretization and historicizing of the Inka origin myth. What *is* clear, however, are Rodrigo Sutiq Callapiña's motives in soliciting their testimony; for with it, he successfully argued his claim to noble status and thereby received exemption from paying taxes and performing public labor and personal service, as well as (presumably) experiencing a considerable boost in personal prestige in both Pacariqtambo and Cuzco.

This is one of many examples in which Andean peoples, through their skillful use of "traditional" mythology, began to act on colonial administrative procedures and effect movements within the newly imposed dominant institutions and bureaucratic structures. We will find in the next section that a similar process of the appropriation of imperial mythology into provincial genealogical history occurred in the case of Rodrigo Sutiq Callapiña's claim to noble descent through his mother.

Kilaku Yupanki Inka and Qoya Qori Kuka in Inka Mythohistory

Concerning Rodrigo Sutiq Callapiña's claims to nobility from his maternal ancestors (fig. 1), we find that Rodrigo did not trace his own matriline, but rather the patriline of his mother, Angelina Qori Qoyllur (Coricoyllor). He claimed that Qori Qoyllur's paternal grandparents, Kilaku Yupanki Inka and Qoya Qori Kuka, were members of the Inka nobility. The two, who lived in the pre-Hispanic era, are referred to in the Callapiña Document as *"gentiles,"* a term that indicates that they died without having been baptized. There is a difference of opinion in two of the testimonies given in 1569 concerning when this couple lived; one version states that it was at the time of Wayna Qhapaq; the other says that they lived at the time of Wayna Qhapaq's son, Waskar Inka.

The second version of the origin myth translated earlier states that Kilaku Yupanki Inka was a member of Caruacalla ayllu. This was an *ayllu* of the upper moiety in Pacariqtambo whose home territory was adjacent to the ruins of Maukallaqta and near Pachecti and Pumaurqu (map 2). As mentioned in chapter 2, Maukallaqta was probably the original site of Pacariqtambo; Pumaurqu was the probable site of Tampu T'oqo; and Pachecti was the first place where the Inka ancestors stopped upon leaving Tampu T'oqo. Therefore, by identifying Kilaku Yupanki Inka as a member of Caruacalla ayllu in Pacariqtambo, Rodrigo made clear to those who were familiar with the geography of the origin place that his great-grandfather was indeed well situated in local and imperial mythic and political space. Furthermore, the second account states that Kilaku was of the "royal blood and generation of the Inkas," and that in the time of Waskar Inka—"before the general reduction"—Kilaku was respected and honored by the Inkas in all of the towns around Cuzco (Appendix, p. 137). As Kilaku was regarded by the Cuzqueñan nobility as an *"Ynga Principal,"* he must have been ranked at least as a member of the provincial seminobility (i.e., the Inkas-by-Privilege) in Inka times. However, certain data to be discussed below suggest that Kilaku may have been of even higher rank.

In a recent study of a "mythstory" recorded by Cabello Valboa (1951 [1586]: 364, 408–416), Robert Randall has argued that two of the characters in that account may be identified with individuals who appear in Rodrigo Sutiq Callapiña's genealogy as described in the Callapiña Document (Randall, *n.d.*).[5] The story from Cabello Valboa concerns the coronation of Waskar Inka, one of two sons of Wayna Qhapaq (the other was Atawallpa) who were contending to succeed their father on the Inka throne. Atawallpa, who was in Quito at the time, sent a messenger named Kilaku Yupanki to attend Waskar's coronation and wedding in Cuzco. Near Cuzco, Kilaku met and fell in love with a woman named Qori Qoyllur, who was the daughter of Waskar Inka. According to Cabello Valboa, Kilaku Yupanki was the son of a man named Awki Thupaq Yupanki and an unnamed woman of the tribe that ruled Quito, the "Quilacos." As Awki Thupaq Yupanki was the full brother of the Inka Wayna Qhapaq, his son, Kilaku, was therefore a foster brother to both Waskar and Atawallpa. As Randall points out, Kilaku Yupanki's "legitimacy as Inka was so pure that he was second only to the Inka [Waskar] himself" (Randall, *n.d.*).

What is interesting in these data for our purposes is that the names of two of the central characters in this mythohistory—Kilaku Yupanki and Qori Qoyllur—are also mentioned in Rodrigo Sutiq Callapiña's genealogy. Angelina Qori Qoyllur was Rodrigo's mother; Kilaku Yupanki Inka was his mother's father's father (fig. 1). By asserting his claim to descent from both Kilaku Yupanki and a woman named Qori Qoyllur, Rodrigo Sutiq Callapiña appears to have been claiming pure royal blood on his matriline. In fact, the combined force of all Rodrigo's claims, which were substantiated by the members of the Inka nobility who served as his witnesses, was to make himself a descendant of the *first* Inka—Manqo Qhapaq—as well as of the *last* undisputed Inka—Wayna Qhapaq. In turning to another of Rodrigo's presumed lineal ascendants, Qoya Qori Kuka (the wife of Kilaku Yupanki Inka), we will find that his claims to descent from this woman appear to have placed him in an indirect line of descent from yet another Inka king, one who has traditionally been a central figure in historicized representations of Inka mythohistory, Pachakuti Inka.

The Matrilineage of the Qori Kukas in Inka Mythohistory

We are told even less in the Callapiña Document about Rodrigo's great-grandmother, Qoya Qori Kuka than about her husband, Kilaku Yupanki Inka. However, there are intriguing data from several of the Spanish chronicles that allow us to suggest a link between Qoya Qori Kuka and a famous woman in Inka mythohistory who bore this same surname, Chañan Qori Kuka. After a discussion of the place of Chañan Qori Kuka in Inka mythohistory, I will return to a consideration of the relationship between Chañan and Qoya Qori Kuka.

Chañan Qori Kuka was an important figure in the principal Inka myth that describes the defense, consolidation, and expansion of the empire under the ninth Inka king, Pachakuti Inka. The central, precipitating event in this set of processes was the war between the Inkas and the Chankas. In outline form, and paraphrasing Sarmiento's version (1942 [1572]: 83–91), the story of the Chanka war goes as follows:

> At the time of the Inka Wiraqocha, the eighth Inka king, there lived to the west of Cuzco a very warlike people, called the Chankas. The Chankas sent word to Inka Wiraqocha that they were going to come and conquer the valley of Cuzco. Wiraqocha, who was old and tired, took fright at this threat and retired to a town to the east of Cuzco, leaving his principal son, Pachakuti Inka, in charge of the defense of the city.
>
> The Chankas attacked Cuzco, splitting their army into three divisions. The Inkas were hard-pressed to defend themselves. The Chankas who attacked Cuzco from the south were firmly repelled by people from the villages of Choco and Cachona, two neighboring towns to the south of Cuzco. The people of Choco and Cachona were led by a courageous and fierce woman named Chañan Curycoca (Chañan Qori Kuka). The tide of the battle began to turn against the Chankas, and they soon retreated. The Chankas attacked a second time and were again beaten back. After a third and final attack—during which the Inkas were aided by stones that turned into warriors (the *pururuna*, or *pururawka*)—the Chankas were thoroughly defeated. After his de-

fense of the city, Pachakuti Inka took over the throne from his father; there followed a massive reorganization and expansion of the Inka state under Pachakuti Inka.

The story of the war with the Chankas represented one of the pivotal events in Inka notions of statehood and dynastic succession (see Duviols, 1980; Rostworowski, 1983; Urbano, 1981; Zuidema, 1973). One of the principal characters in the defense of Cuzco in the accounts of the Chanka war was Chañan Qori Kuka, the fierce woman warrior from Choco and Cachona. In addition to Sarmiento de Gamboa's reference to this woman, the chronicler Pachacuti Yamqui also mentions a woman—a "widow"—named Chhañancoricoca, who fought with the Inkas against the Chankas and a group called the Hancoallos (Pachacuti Yamqui, 1950 [1613]: 238).[6]

Chañan Qori Kuka must have been an exceptionally important figure in the post-conquest written and oral traditions of the circum-Cuzco region. This is suggested by the fact that she is the central figure in a painting that now hangs in the Museo de Arqueología y Antropología in Cuzco (plate 5). The painting is rendered in the famous Cuzco style and probably dates to the latter part of the seventeenth or early eighteenth century (see Mesa and Gisbert, 1982: 172–183, 283–287). We do not know when this painting was made, nor do we know by whom it was painted. However, given what we *do* know about Chañan Qori Kuka from references to her in the Spanish chronicles, it is likely that the painting depicts her holding the decapitated head of a Chanka warrior, on whose body she stands. I would surmise that the man who stands to her right is Pachakuti Inka. The reason for including a reproduction of this painting of Chañan Qori Kuka here is to emphasize, first, that this woman was quite a famous figure in Inka mythohistory, and second, that some knowledge about, and appreciation of, her role in relation to warfare and (presumably) royalty was current in the Cuzco area in the seventeenth century.

Chañan Qori Kuka may well have represented more than an incidental character in an Inka myth. I would hypothesize that this woman may have been a member, perhaps the founding ancestress, of a matrilineage of noblewomen to the south of Cuzco, the surname, or title, of which would have been Qori Kuka (golden coca). The word *chañan* (or *chanan*) itself suggests that this woman may have represented a lineage. González Holguín glosses *chananmittan* as "lineage," "caste," or "one's descendants including children and grandchildren" (1952 [1608]: 77). Rostworowski (1983: 136–137, and n. 27) has raised the possibility, specifically in relation to Chañan

Plate 5. "The Great Princess Chañan Coricoca," Museo de Arqueología, Cuzco. Photo by R. Tom Zuidema

Qori Kuka, that there may have been a matrilineal *ayllu* of royal women to the south of Cuzco, in the area of Choco and Cachona. Qoya Qori Kuka, the great-grandmother of Rodrigo Sutiq Callapiña and the wife of Kilaku Yupanki Inka, may have been a member of this hypothetical matrilineage. I would note in passing another possible member, one who would have established a further link between Pacariqtambo and the Inka nobility. Sinchi Ruq'a, the son of Manqo Qhapaq and Mama Oqllu who was born within the territory of Pacariqtambo, later married a woman named Mama Kuka (Qori Kuka?). Mama Kuka was from the village of Sañu, the fifth *ayllu* of the lower moiety of Cuzco (Sarmiento, 1942 [1572]:63).

That the woman Chañan Qori Kuka was an important figure in Inka ideology and mythohistory is further attested to by the existence of a sacred stone within the valley of Cuzco that was called Chañan Curi Coca. The chronicler Bernabé Cobo describes this stone as a "sacred place" (*waka*); this was one of the *pururawkas*—a rock that turned into a (female) warrior—who helped Pachakuti Inka defend Cuzco against the Chankas (1964 [1653]: 184). Chañan Qori Kuka was at the nexus of a complex set of important genealogical, political, and territorial relationships in Inka mythohistory. In order to understand the significance of this character in the Chanka war and as a sacred stone in the valley of Cuzco, as well as to situate both Chañan and Qoya Qori Kuka in the relations between Cuzco and ethnic groups to the south of the city, it is necessary to describe briefly the social and territorial organizations of Inka Cuzco. An additional objective of this description is to define the "south," from the point of view of Cuzco, in more precise geopolitical and mythohistorical terms.

The Place of Chañan Qori Kuka in the Ceque System of Cuzco

The organization of Inka Cuzco was based on a system of forty-one imaginary "lines," called *ceques*, which radiated out like the spokes of a wheel from the temple of Qorikancha (golden enclosure) in the center of the city. Each *ceque* joined a linear series of sacred places (*wakas*) in a different direction from the temple of Qorikancha to the horizon. The forty-one *ceques* were grouped into quadrants, called *suyus*; the quadrants were paired to form moieties, called *sayas*. The quadrant that included the area from the southeast to the southwest of the valley of Cuzco was called Kuntisuyu. Kuntisuyu and Qollasuyu together made up the southern moiety (Hurincuzco); Chinchaysuyu and Antisuyu composed the northern moiety, Hanancuzco (Cobo, 1964 [1653]: 63–66; Zuidema, 1964: 2–5). There were nine *ceques* in three of the quadrants and fourteen in the fourth (Kuntisuyu). The *ceques* within each quadrant were ranked in repeating sequences of three hierarchical categories: 1 = *qollana*; 2 = *payan*; 3 = *kayao*.

The *ceque* system's organization of the space of the valley of Cuzco was linked to the sociopolitical organization of the capital in the following way. The population of Cuzco was organized into ten royal *ayllus*, called *panaqas*, and ten nonroyal *ayllus*. In Inka mythohistory, each *panaqa* was considered to have been composed of the descendants of an Inka king with the exception of his successor, who formed his own *panaqa*. The ten nonroyal *ayllus* had their supposed origins all at one time; that is, these *ayllus* were created by the Inka ancestors from among the Tambos Indians who lived around Tampu T'oqo. The hierarchical position of each of the twenty *ayllus* was indicated by its association with a particular *ceque*, quadrant, and moiety as well as by the representations of the origin and deeds of the ancestors of the *ayllu* in the collective mythohistory of the empire.

The *ceques* defining the boundaries of the quadrants of the city of Cuzco were conceptually extended from the valley of Cuzco to the limits of the empire in the four directions. This extension of the boundaries of the quadrants provided the basis for the division of the empire into four quarters, a principle that found its expression in the name applied by the Inkas to the empire as a whole—Tawantin-suyu (four parts). Therefore, beyond the boundaries of Cuzco, the southern quadrant, Kuntisuyu, included the villages of Choco and Cachona as well as Pacariqtambo (Zuidema and Poole, 1982). Pacariqtambo lies almost straight south of Cuzco.

There are two issues concerning the organization of Cuzco that can provide us with insights into the role of the hypothetical matrilineage of the Qori Kukas in the *ceque* system and in the geopolitical organization of provincial social and territorial groups as determined by the extension of the boundaries of the *ceque* system beyond the valley of Cuzco. The first of these concerns the status of the *ceque* (line) that pointed straight south from the temple of Qorikancha; the second concerns the role of the noblewomen from Kuntisuyu in Inka sociopolitical organization.

In his chronicle, Bernabé Cobo gives the name and, in most cases, a brief description of each of the sacred sites that made up the forty-one *ceques* of the *ceque* system. A number of *ceques* in Kuntisuyu (the southern quadrant) included sacred sites that were identified with people, places, or events of the origin myth. For instance, the first sacred site on each of two *ceques* that went south-southeast from the Qorikancha is explicitly associated in Cobo's account with the ancestors and Pacariqtambo. The first of these (*ceque* IV_B1c in Zuidema's notation), which was the *ceque* associated with the royal *ayllu* of the first Inka king, Manqo Qhapaq (i.e., Chimapanaqa), is described by Cobo as follows: "The first [*waka*] they called Caritam-pucancha. It was a small plaza that is now within the convent of Santo Domingo, of which they held the opinion that it was the place where Manco Capac first settled in Cuzco after he left Tampu. Children and all other things are offered [as sacrifices to this *waka*]" (Cobo, 1964 [1653]: 184).

Of the *ceque* that pointed just to the east of south (*ceque* IV_B1a),

Cobo says the following: "The first [*waka*] was a small house called Inticancha, in which they said lived the sisters of the first Inca who emerged with him from the window of Pacaritampu. They sacrificed children to this [*waka*]" (Cobo, 1964 [1653]: 184).

And finally, the first *waka* of the *ceque* that pointed straight south from Cuzco (*ceque* IV$_A$3a,c), which was adjacent to the *ceque* just described, is identified by Cobo as follows: "The first [*waka*] was called Chañan Curi Coca. It was a rock that they say turned into a woman who came with the *pururaucas*" (Cobo, 1964 [1653]: 184).[7]

The two *wakas* described in the first two passages fix the place of the Inka ancestors within the overall sociopolitical, spatial, and temporal organization of Cuzco. These places represent a "concretization" of the ancestors within the political geography of the valley of Cuzco. By their *ceque* affiliations, the sacred places identified with the ancestors were associated with populations and social groups located to the south of Cuzco, within the quadrant of Kuntisuyu. As we are concerned here primarily with the role of Chañan Qori Kuka in the *ceque* system, I will turn to a consideration of the *waka* and *ceque* with which this woman was identified, that is, the first *waka* of the *ceque* that pointed straight south from Cuzco (*ceque* IV$_A$3a,c).

The *ceque* on which the rock called Chañan Qori Kuka was located was important for a number of reasons. As noted, this alignment of *wakas* went straight south from Cuzco. As such, the *ceque* defined an important spatial and temporal boundary marker in Inka cosmology, for this was the direction from Cuzco to the region of the sky where the Inka constellations of the Southern Cross and the "eyes of the Llama" (α and β Centauri) had their upper culmination at midnight around the time of the September equinox. The upper culmination at midnight of these two constellations occurred at the height of the planting season in the Cuzco Valley, and these constellations were closely observed in the correlation of the solar, lunar, and stellar periodicities that made up the Inka ritual calendar (Urton, 1981, 1986; Zuidema, 1982a, 1986; Zuidema and Urton, 1976). Taken in conjunction with the direction to the point on the horizon in the southeast from where these stars were seen to rise (i.e., *ceque* IV$_B$3b), these two *ceques* defined the spatial and calendrical boundaries of an area that was associated in Inka ideology and mythohistory with the autochthonous, non-Inkaic populations of the valley of Cuzco, as well as with the Inkas-by-Privilege outside Cuzco. These populations were represented in Inka mythohistory as sources of fecundity and prosperity (Zuidema, 1986: 96–98).

The links between the Inka nobility and the two groups mentioned earlier were mediated through women, especially women in the quadrant of Kuntisuyu. In the case of the autochthonous populations, these links to the Inka nobility were formed by divine ancestral females, including the four ancestresses who emerged from Tampu T'oqo at the time of creation; Pachamama (earth/time mother); and Mama Anawarki. The latter name (or title) referred both to a mountain to the south of Cuzco that was worshiped by the autochthonous populations in Cuzco, and to the wife of Pachakuti Inka, a woman from the village of Choco (Sarmiento, 1942 [1572]: 99; Zuidema, 1986:97–98).

The connections between the Inkas-by-Privilege and the Inka nobility in Cuzco were established by the marriage of these provincial semielites to the female nobility of Cuzco. In the quadrant of Kuntisuyu, these royal women were known by the special name *iñaqa*. The word *iñaqa* was also used more broadly to refer to the sisters of the Inka who were given as wives to the lords (*kurakas*) of forty thousand, twenty thousand, and ten thousand households throughout the empire (Zuidema, 1986:89). I would suggest that the two women with whom we are principally concerned here, Chañan Qori Kuka and Qoya Qori Kuka, were probably both women of the *iñaqa* class, the former because of her central role (as an outside woman) in the defense of Cuzco against the Chankas, the latter because of her title (*qoya,* "queen") and because of her marriage to an *"Ynga Principal"*—Kilaku Yupanki Inka—of Pacariqtambo.

"Iñaqa" was a key term and concept in Inka sociopolitical organization. For example, the system of ranking the royal *ayllus* (*panaqas*) in Cuzco may have had its origin in the ranking of the ten age grades of both the *iñaqas* and the "Virgins of the Sun" (Zuidema, 1986:73, 88–89; see also Alberti M., 1985:558, 570–572; Rostworowski, 1983:142–143). We should recall in this connection that in Sarmiento de Gamboa's version of the origin myth, the hierarchy of *ages* among the four ancestral sisters who emerged from the cave of Tampu T'oqo appears to have provided the model and basis for the hierarchy of *authority* among the four brothers. In the ranking of royal *ayllus* in Cuzco, the highest-ranking *panaqa* was called both Hatun Ayllu and Iñaqa Panaqa. This was the royal *ayllu* of Pachakuti Inka, the name (or title) associated in Inka mythohistory not only with the defense of Cuzco against the Chankas and the subsequent consolidation and expansion of the empire, but also with the heroic woman Chañan Qori Kuka.

Through the various data and lines of argument just outlined, we are able to link the names of Chañan Qori Kuka and Qoya Qori Kuka with Pachakuti Inka and his royal *ayllu,* Hatun Ayllu/Iñaqa Panaqa.

Rostworowski, in fact, has argued explicitly that Iñaqa Panaqa may have been a matrilineal *ayllu* that was composed primarily of noble-women, that is, *iñaqas* (1983:143). Iñaqa Panaqa could have been the *ayllu* with which the hypothetical matrilineage of the "Qori Kukas" described earlier was affiliated.

The connection between Chañan Qori Kuka and Pachakuti Inka is made clearly in the mythohistorical accounts of the war with the Chankas. What is crucial to recognize here is that through his own deeds, Pachakuti Inka himself formed the link between Chañan Qori Kuka and the great-grandmother of Rodrigo Sutiq Callapiña, Qoya Qori Kuka. This link was formed by Pachakuti Inka in the following way. One of the first acts he undertook after taking over the throne from his father was to "return," as it were, to Pacariqtambo and enter the cave of Tampu T'oqo. Sarmiento gives the following account of this event: "As he [Pachakuti Inka] was curious to know about ancient things, and in order to perpetuate his name, he went personally to the mountain of *Tambo-toco or Pacariqtambo, which is all one thing*, and entered the cave where they know for certain Manco Capac and his siblings emerged when they first went to Cuzco" (Sarmiento, 1942 [1572]:93; my emphasis.)

With this act, Pachakuti Inka established links among a number of central characters, events, and categories of people of Inka cosmology. These links included the following: (1) the founding of the empire under Manqo Qhapaq with its defense, consolidation, and expansion under Pachakuti Inka; (2) the ten non-royal *ayllus* of Cuzco—whose origins were in Tampu T'oqo—and Pachakuti Inka's own royal *ayllu*, Hatun Ayllu/Iñaqa Panaqa; and (3) *iñaqa* women of Pacariqtambo with those elsewhere in Kuntisuyu and throughout the empire. The last is personified, in the material discussed here, by the relationship, concretized in Pachakuti Inka's visit to Tampu T'oqo, between Chañan Qori Kuka and Qoya Qori Kuka, two *iñaqa* women of Kuntisuyu.

It is curious to note in connection with the latter point that the chronicler Blas Valera, writing in about 1590 (1950:166), refers to Pachakuti Inka as "Señor de Pacari Tampu" (lord of Pacariqtambo). This title suggests that Blas Valera may have been aware of some tradition by which Pachakuti Inka, like Manqo Qhapaq as portrayed in the Chronicle of the *Khipukamayuqs*, was considered to have been a native lord (*kuraka*) of the place of origin. Through his association with Chañan Qori Kuka in the myth of the Chanka war, and in his subsequent visit to Pacariqtambo, Pachakuti Inka appears to have had a particularly close relationship to the Qori Kuka matrilineage of *iñaqas* in the quadrant of Kuntisuyu.

Summary

We can now return with this larger perspective on local and regional genealogical history to the case of Rodrigo Sutiq Callapiña. It is in the context of the mythohistorical relationships analyzed in the foregoing that we must situate Rodrigo's claims to descent from Manqo Qhapaq, Kilaku Yupanki Inka, and Qoya Qori Kuka. It must be stressed that the last three were *all* mythohistorical characters who supposedly lived in pre-Hispanic—that is, "prehistoric"—times. The identities of these characters are the products of the recollections and ideological constructions of people who were called on by the Spanish to testify concerning these individuals for a variety of purposes (e.g., from the determination of the juridical status of individuals to the reconstruction of Inka history). The informants were working from a well-known body of mythohistorical traditions and they were reinterpreting those traditions within colonial Spanish hierarchical relations and bureaucratic structures (see Duviols, 1977; MacCormack, 1984; Rostworowski, 1983; Zuidema, 1986).

This is not to say, however, that Rodrigo Sutiq Callapiña and the Inka noblemen who testified in his behalf necessarily fabricated the lines of descent illustrated in figure 1. Rodrigo's purported noble ancestors, including Manqo Qhapaq, may well have represented an established nexus of genealogical and ideological relationships in Inka mythohistory between elites in Cuzco and Pacariqtambo in pre-Hispanic times. However, I would argue that the statuses, if not the actual identities, of the ancestors of Rodrigo Sutiq Callapiña—a *cacique principal* from Pacariqtambo—were at least to some degree *prefigured* in the local and regional mythohistorical traditions shared by all of those involved in the legal proceeding of 1569, save for the Spaniards who were recording the testimony and adjudicating the case. The genealogical identities and connections were prefigured in the sense that a discourse about the ancestry of a member of the elite *in Pacariqtambo* would, of political, social, and mythohistorical necessity, have evoked certain categories and relationships (e.g., ancestors and *iñaqas*), if not particular identities (i.e., Manqo Qhapaq, Pachakuti Inka, and the matrilineage of the Qori Kukas).

The effect of the testimony recorded in the 1569 proceedings in the Callapiña Document was to *reinterpret* categories and relations that once had meaning in the context, for instance, of the *ceque* system of Cuzco in terms of the categories and relations of the Spanish colonial world. The knowledge of, and ability to use, such shared traditions as that described above as a basis for argumentation during the colonial period represented one of the tactics whereby the conquered populations of the Cuzco area, and those elsewhere in the Andes, confronted, and at times successfully manipulated, the colonial bureaucracy (see de Certeau, 1984, on the general nature of what he calls "tactical" appropriations by subordinate populations of institutions and policies imposed by dominant societies; for excellent examples of the implementation of such appropriations in the Andes, see Adorno, 1986 : 13–32; Silverblatt, 1981 : 317–322; Stern, 1982*a* : 114–137).

The postconquest legal and historical discourses that were incorporated into the Spanish chronicles began to give shape and concrete form to the substance of pre-Hispanic mythohistory. The assertions that were made concerning family histories in such proceedings as those recorded in the Callapiña Document played an important, cumulative role in the formulation not only of concrete representations of local genealogical relations and institutional structures in pre-Hispanic times, but also of the presumed nature of historical causality within the empire as a whole.

Historicizing the Origin Myth: The Cast of Characters

The discussions of the Chronicle of the *Khipukamayuqs* and the Callapiña Document in previous sections established two points concerning the early colonial history of the production of the Inka origin myth. First, the place of "Pacariqtambo" was transformed *in the written testimony* during the period from 1542 to 1569 from a geographically undefined place to a specific community, some of whose residents and social groups were identified in legal documents as descendants of Manqo Qhapaq. And second, it appears both from the chronicles and from the historical documents from Pacariqtambo that one especially prominent family of *caciques principales*, the Callapiñas, played a central role in the production and manipulation of historicized representations of the origin myth. In this section, I will examine the identities of certain elite individuals in Cuzco who also appear to have participated in the formulation of historicized versions of the Inka origin myth and who, in the process, were also partially responsible for delimiting the geography of the place of origin in the Spanish chronicles.

That the Callapiña family was influential and highly respected throughout the communities to the south of Cuzco, and in Cuzco itself, is attested to most forcefully by the testimony given in behalf of Rodrigo Sutiq Callapiña in 1569 by eight descendants of Inka nobility in Cuzco. When we look more closely at who these men were, we confront the rather startling circumstance that several of them

Table 3. Coincidences among Witnesses in Three Colonial Legal Proceedings

Witnesses for Rodrigo Sutiq Callapiña (May 2, 1569)	Selected Witnesses for the Descendants of Thupa Inka Yupanki (May 9, 1569)	Selected Witnesses for Sarmiento de Gamboa (1572)
Diego Atao Yupanqui (age 85)	Santiago Auca Mirar (age 90) [Hanancuzco]	
Santiago Aucamira (age 93)		
Domingo Pascac (age 98)		Domingo Pascac (age 90) [Hatun Ayllu/Iñaqa Panaqa]
Francisco Rauraua (age 106)	Juan Picarro Yupanqui (age 86) [Hanancuzco, Parish of Belén]	Juan Pizarro Yupanqui [Arayraka Ayllu Cuzco-Kallan]
Juan Pissarro Yupanqui (age 120)		
Gonzalo Llamac Auca Ynga (age 94)		Gonzalo Ampura Llama Oca [Maras Ayllo]
Martín Natipi Yupanqui (age 132)	Martín Nadpe Yupanqui (age 86) [Hanancuzco]	
Francisco Apuranti (age 108)		

were also witnesses in other proceedings that were going on in Cuzco at about the same time; the net result of the activities of these individuals was the production of a body of testimony from which some of the first "official" and thoroughly historicized versions of Inka mythohistory were produced.

On May 2, 1569, the eight men who are identified as witnesses in the Callapiña Document (note 4) appeared before Licenciado Juan Ayllon in Cuzco to give testimony in behalf of Rodrigo Sutiq Callapiña concerning Manqo Qhapaq's origin from Pacariqtambo (see Appendix, p. 129). One week later, on May 9, Juan Ayllon received testimony from ten witnesses concerning the descendants of Thupa Inka Yupanki, the son of Pachakuti Inka and the father of the last undisputed Inka king, Wayna Qhapaq (Rowe, 1985b: 221). Three of the witnesses for this latter proceeding had also testified the week before for Rodrigo Sutiq Callapiña. And finally, at what must have been around this same time, Sarmiento de Gamboa was collecting testimony on the history and customs of the Inkas from members of the royal and nonroyal *ayllus* in Cuzco. Three of Sarmiento's informants also served as witnesses in the Callapiña proceeding; one of the three, Juan Pizarro (Pissarro) Yupanqui, had served as well as a witness in the proceeding to identify the descendants of Thupa Inka Yupanki (Rowe, 1985b: 237–238). The coincidences in the witnesses who testified in the three proceedings are shown in table 3.

Although we do not have extensive biographical information on any one of the witnesses identified in table 3, it is particularly instructive to discuss what is known about one of the witnesses in some detail (Domingo Pascac), and of two others in passing (Juan Pizarro Yupanqui and Gonzalo Ampura Llama Oca). The purpose of these discussions is to stress the point that the legal proceeding involving Rodrigo Sutiq Callapiña was part of a larger process—and perhaps, given its timing, even a *precipitating* event—in which elites in Cuzco and the provinces set about to establish the nobility of their lineages. It is likely that one of the principal factors motivating this activity was the recognition on the part of the indigenous elites in the circum-Cuzco region of the need to secure their positions in the restructuring and reorganization of the native population that was being initiated at this time by Francisco de Toledo.

As stated earlier, Viceroy Toledo charged Sarmiento with the task of compiling a history of the Inka empire as a basis for his (Toledo's) reorganization of the colony. Toledo saw to it that Sarmiento had at his disposal all of the resources and information necessary to complete this task. Thus, Sarmiento was able to interview more than one hundred *khipukamayuqs* (1942 [1572]: 176–179). Upon the completion of his history, Sarmiento brought together forty-two no-tables, all of whom were residents of Cuzco and descendants of the royal *ayllus* (*panaqas*) of Cuzco, to affirm the veracity of his ac-count. These forty-two men are identified by name, age, and *panaqa* affiliation at the end of Sarmiento's chronicle (these identifications were recorded by Toledo's scribe, Alvaro Ruiz de Navamuel; Sar-miento, 1942 [1572]: 175–181).

The oldest informant among the forty-two men assembled by Sar-miento was a ninety-year-old named Domingo Pascac. Pascac identi-fied himself as a member of Pachakuti Inka's royal *ayllu, Hatun Ayllu/Iñaqa Panaqa* (Sarmiento, 1942 [1572]: 178). As we know from the Callapiña Document, one of the witnesses who testified in behalf of Rodrigo Sutiq Callapiña was a ninety-eight-year-old man also named Domingo Pascac. Pascac is identified in the Callapiña Document as a resident of the Parish of San Blas in Cuzco (Appen-dix, p. 133).

There is an eleven-year discrepancy in the ages of the "Domingo Pascacs" identified in these two documents. That is, if Domingo Pascac was 98 years old in 1569 when he testified in behalf of Rodrigo Sutiq Callapiña, then when he testified before Sarmiento three years later, in 1572, he should have been 101 years old; instead, Sar-miento's scribe recorded Domingo Pascac's age as 90. I do not find this eleven-year discrepancy to be a sufficiently compelling reason to think that the two accounts might refer to different men. It is highly unlikely, I think, that between 1569 and 1572 there were two men in Cuzco over 90 and named Domingo Pascac who were well-enough regarded by both the Spanish and the Inka nobility to have been called on to give testimony on the history and genealogy of the Inkas. When Domingo Pascac reported his age on these two occa-sions, he was no doubt concerned primarily with indicating that he was an "old man" and, therefore, that he was someone who should be respected and listened to.[8]

There is, in fact, a third reference to what I would interpret as a single individual named Domingo Pascac. This reference comes from a document written on 14 February 1572. It concerns a set of four tapestries (*paños*) showing the origin and descent of the Inka kings that were made in the early 1570s. The tapestries were pro-duced for the king of Spain, Philip II, at the behest of Viceroy Toledo, to illustrate the genealogy of the Inka kings (the tapestries have never come to light).

Before sending the tapestries to Spain, Toledo called together thirty-seven descendants of Inka nobility in Cuzco to testify as to the veracity of the "history" of the Inkas as represented in them.

Among the witnesses was a man named, simply, "don Domingo"; don Domingo was said to be ninety-nine years old and a member of the *panaqa* of Pachakuti Inka (Iwasaki Cauti, 1986:72–73). The scribe who recorded this information was Alvaro Ruiz de Navamuel, the same man who, on 29 February 1572, recorded the identification of a ninety-year-old man named Domingo Pascac as one of the informants who testified to the veracity of Sarmiento de Gamboa's *Historia de los Incas*. When we add this third reference to "don Domingo" of the *panaqa* of Pachakuti Inka to the other two shown in table 3, it would seem to me to strain reasonable limits of incredulity to suppose that they do *not* all identify the same man. I will proceed on the assumption that the person named Domingo Pascac who testified in behalf of Rodrigo Sutiq Callapiña in 1569 was the same person identified in the proceedings convened by Viceroy Toledo and Sarmiento de Gamboa in the early 1570s.

Therefore, Sarmiento's oldest informant on the Inka origin myth had testified to the Spanish three years earlier that Manqo Qhapaq had come from Pacariqtambo, that he (Manqo Qhapaq) was the ancestor of the Callapiñas, a family of *caciques principales* who lived there. I cannot trace any genealogical or other connection between Domingo Pascac and Rodrigo Sutiq Callapiña that might provide a motive for why the former testified in behalf of the latter. Nor is it clear why, if he did *not* think it was the case, Domingo Pascac's testimony in the Callapiña Document concretized the origin place of Manqo Qhapaq to the town of Pacariqtambo and the lineage of the Callapiñas.

The critical point about Domingo Pascac's testimony in 1569 in the context of the larger problem of the concretization of the origin myth is that among Sarmiento's forty-two informants, Domingo Pascac was one of eight men who were descendants of the *panaqa* of Pachakuti Inka (Hatun Ayllu/Iñaqa Panaqa). This *panaqa* affiliation is important for the problems under consideration here because Pachakuti Inka himself was considered to have been particularly interested in the history of the empire. Pachakuti Inka was said to have compiled the history of the Inkas who lived before him (Sarmiento, 1942 [1572]:180); for this purpose, he regularly called provincial *khipukamayuqs* to the court in Cuzco to recount the traditions of the "antiquities, origin, and notable things" of the ancestors of their peoples (Sarmiento, 1942 [1572]:46).

It may well be the case, as Zuidema has argued (1982c:173–174; 1986:64–66, 103), that the Inka kings were not historical personages at all, but rather that they were the personifications of titled political statuses and bureaucratic offices that became historicized in the postconquest constructions of Inka "history." Nonetheless, because of the traits and interests that were attributed to "Pachakuti Inka" in the mythohistorical traditions that were shared by the descendants of the Inka nobility in the early colonial period, Sarmiento's informants probably associated this name, or title, with the official history of the Inkas. Therefore, the descendants of Pachakuti Inka in Hatun Ayllu/Iñaqa Panaqa would probably have been considered the legitimate historians of the empire. As one of the oldest members of Pachakuti Inka's *panaqa* in Cuzco in the early 1570s, Domingo Pascac would have been recognized as one of the highest authorities on Inka "history."

In addition, if, as suggested earlier, Pachakuti Inka *did* have a special relationship to the matrilineage of Qori Kuka within the class of *iñaqas*, then this relationship would presumably have held for his descendants as well. If this were the case, we could therefore understand why Domingo Pascac might have placed Chañan Qori Kuka in a special relationship to Pachakuti Inka in the story of the Chanka war and the return of Pachakuti Inka to the cave of Tampu T'oqo after the war. Domingo Pascac's testimony in behalf of Rodrigo Sutiq Callapiña in 1569, in which he confirmed the noble status of Rodrigo's great-grandmother, Qoya Qori Kuka, should be seen as an earlier elaboration, given in the context of the reconstruction of a particular genealogical history in Pacariqtambo, of the role and privileged status of women of the surname Qori Kuka in the disposition of *iñaqas* and Inkas-by-Privilege in the circum-Cuzco region in pre-Hispanic times.

We should consider here as well the identities of two of the other witnesses who testified jointly for Rodrigo Sutiq Callapiña in 1569. The two men in question were Juan Pizarro Yupanqui and Gonzalo Llamac Auca Ynga; both of these men are identified in the Callapiña Document as residents of the Parish of Belén in Cuzco (Appendix, p. 134; see also n. 4). We know something further concerning the identities of these two men from Sarmiento's chronicle. In his identification of the living members of the nonroyal *ayllus* of Cuzco, Sarmiento states that Juan Pizarro Yupanqui was a member of Arayraka Ayllo Cuzco-Kallan and that a man named Gonzalo Ampura Llama Oca was a member of Maras Ayllo (1942 [1572]:50–51). Sarmiento does not state whether or not he used these two men as informants. However, it seems likely that he would have done so, given that he was interested in the history of both the royal *and* the nonroyal *ayllus*, and that he specifically identifies these two men as members of two of the nonroyal *ayllus*. In addition, we know that Juan Pizarro Yupanqui had served in 1569 as one of the witnesses for the proceeding to establish the noble ancestry of the descendants of Thupa Inka Yupanki (see table 3).

The only difficulty in identifying the two men mentioned by Sarmiento with the two witnesses for Rodrigo Sutiq Callapiña is the difference in the name of the second individual: Gonzalo Llamac Auca Ynga (Callapiña Document)/Gonzalo Ampura Llama Oca (Sarmiento). The difference between Auca and Oca can easily be ascribed to an error in transcription. This leaves, however, the difference of the addition of the title "Ynga" in the first recording of the name and of the addition of the surname Ampura in the second. As I argued in relation to the differences in the recorded ages of the two Domingo Pascacs, I find it unlikely that there were two men with virtually the same name in Cuzco from 1569 to 1572 who would both have been highly enough respected to have been called on to testify in such proceedings as those that we are discussing here. Therefore, I would propose as a hypothesis that the two names— Gonzalo Llamac Auca Ynga and Gonzalo Ampura Llama Oca— identify the same man.

The *ayllu* affiliations of Juan Pizarro Yupanqui and Gonzalo (Ampura) Llamac Auca/Oca (Ynga) are of interest for the following reasons. Arayraka Ayllu Cuzco-Kallan, the *ayllu* affiliation of Juan Pizarro Yupanqui, was the second *ayllu* of the upper moiety of Cuzco (see table 2). The ancestor of Arayraka Ayllu Cuzco-Kallan was Ayar Uchu, the fourth ancestor-brother who emerged with Manqo Qhapaq from Tampu T'oqo (table 1). This nonroyal *ayllu* was considered one of two that comprised the descendants of the autochthonous populations of the valley of Cuzco, the Allcabizas (Zuidema, 1964 : 194). Maras Ayllu, the second *ayllu* of the lower moiety of Cuzco, was descended from the window of Maras T'oqo, one of the two lateral caves at the site of Tampu T'oqo (Sarmiento, 1942 [1572] : 49–51). Therefore, the *ayllu* affiliations of these two men placed them in positions to represent mythohistorical identities closely associated with the origin place, primordial times, and autochthonous populations in the circum-Cuzco region. The fact that these two men testified in behalf of Rodrigo Sutiq Callapiña further attests to the centrality of this provincial lineage in the mythohistorical traditions and ideology connected with the origin of the empire.

I will conclude by suggesting that Domingo Pascac, Juan Pizarro Yupanqui, and Gonzalo (Ampura) Llamac Auca/Oca (Ynga) appear to have been at least three of the possible sources of the concretization of the place of origin and the historicizing of Inka mythohistory in the account of the origin myth recorded by Sarmiento de Gamboa. Although we have identified a few individuals who may have participated in concretizing the place of origin, we still cannot say whether this represented a transformation or distortion of the nature and space of the origin place from pre-Hispanic traditions. All we can say on the basis of the foregoing is that, first, there was a curious coincidence between the founding of the Spanish-enforced reduction (town) of Pacariqtambo in 1571 and the official concretization of the origin place in Sarmiento's history in 1572; and second, the process of concretizing the origin place seems to have become more pronounced as one goes from the Chronicle of the *Khipu-kamayuqs* in the 1540s, through the Callapiña Document in the 1560s, to Sarmiento de Gamboa's *Historia de los Incas* in the 1570s. That is, the process of the *concretization* of the Inka place of origin proceeded in step with the *historicizing* of Inka mythohistory.

4. Ethnographic and Ethnohistorical Dimensions for a Local Interpretation of the Inka Origin Myth

The Constraints of Ethnographic Analogy

In the previous chapters, we encountered several references to, and representations of, the town or area of Pacariqtambo from the mid- to late 1500s. These references consisted primarily of general statements about this area from an outsider's point of view, or they gave specific information about the geography or social organization of Pacariqtambo, which was not only incomplete and decontextualized but which was presented primarily from the point of view of Cuzco. However, since the origin place of the Inka ancestors *did* become identified with the town of Pacariqtambo by the 1570s, it is essential that we have a clear understanding of the social and political organizations of the small provincial town that was the object of these early colonial mythohistorical, and increasingly historical, representations. Such an understanding will allow us to approach the second question posed in Chapter 1 as one of the objectives of this study. That is, what light can we bring to an interpretation of the Inka origin myth on the basis of an understanding of the community of Pacariqtambo itself?

I will begin this chapter with a description of the contemporary sociopolitical organization of the town and district of Pacariqtambo. The ethnographic data provide the clearest description available to us of the organization of social and territorial groups within the district; therefore, it will be helpful for a clear presentation and interpretation of the historical documents from the community to begin with an ethnographic overview of the area that has been known since the late sixteenth century as Pacariqtambo. Following a discussion of the ethnographic materials, I will turn to the social history of Pacariqtambo as it can be reconstructed from historical documents from the mid- to late sixteenth century. This is the period that is most relevant for our study because it was during this time

Table 4. The Ayllus of Pacariqtambo

1 1568	2 1571	3 1595	4 1792	5 1836	6 1980–1988
Hanansayaq					
Quinuara	Naivapuca	Nayba	Naigua	Nayhua	Nayhua
Acchacara	Quinoaca	Quimbara	Quinuara	Quinhuara	Quinhuara
Caruacalla	Achacari	Acchacari	Acchacar	Acchacara	Aqchakar
Pachicti	Carnacollo	Carbacalla	Carguacaya	Ccarhuacalla	Qarhuacalla 1ro
	Pachete	Pachite	Pachipti	Pachecte	Qarhuacalla 2do
	Marcagalla			Rumiticti	
Hurinsayaq					
Cuño	Cuño	San Miguel	San Miguel	San Miguel	San Miguel
	Guatupasta	Pirca	Pirca	Pirca	P'irca
Cuypa	Aupa	Coypa	Coypa	Ccoypa	Yanchacalla
	Guancho y	Guaycho/	Guaicho	Huaycho	Huaycho
	Anchacalla	Marangalla	Yanchacalla	Huaychacalla	Pumatambo
					(Qoipa)

Note: I can trace references to the moiety division among the *ayllus* only back to 1792.

Sources:

Col. 1. Glave, personal communication; Chap. 4, n. 3.

Col. 2. Ulloa, 1909.

Col. 3. A.M.A., C., Exp. #5877.

Col. 4. A.D.C., *Intendencia, Gobierno.*

Col. 5. A.D.C., *Tesorería Fiscal de Cuzco, Libros de Matrículas,* lib. no. 3, 1836.

Col. 6. Urton, 1984, 1988.

that the origin myths were being recorded in historical and legal documents in Cuzco. Table 4, which contains six lists of the *ayllus* of Pacariqtambo from 1568 to 1988, will serve as the key to the ethnographic and ethnohistorical descriptions and interpretations presented in this chapter.

Before proceeding, two points should be clarified. The first concerns the scope of this inquiry; the second concerns the rationale for including contemporary ethnographic materials in a study that is concerned primarily with the analysis of early colonial-period societies.

The study of sociopolitical organization in Pacariqtambo presented here does not pretend to be exhaustive in historical terms. This will become obvious when I move from the present-day back to the early colonial period without discussing events and processes of social transformation that occurred during the intervening period. For example, this study leaves unexamined such important processes of change as the increasing participation of the community in the market economy beginning in the earliest days of the colony and the inexorable growth of an extensive network of haciendas in this area beginning in the late seventeenth century and continuing until the abrupt (and virtually complete) end of the haciendas with the Agrarian Reform in the early 1970s. Both of these processes had a profound impact on the economic, social, and political organizations in the District of Pacariqtambo (as they did elsewhere in the Andes). For instance, by the beginning of this century, almost one-half of the total land within the District of Pacariqtambo was controlled by the haciendas. The hacienda system was one of the central forces promoting the increasing commercialization of agriculture (e.g., producing wheat and barley for the market in Cuzco), the privatization of landholding, and the relocation of people from Pacariqtambo and surrounding communities to the haciendas (or to villages near the haciendas) to serve as laborers (See Glave, 1986; Hünefeldt, 1982; Mallon, 1983; Poole, 1984).

In many Andean communities, processes such as the foregoing led to the virtual, if not complete, disintegration of local *ayllu* organizations. This has not occurred in Pacariqtambo. The *ayllus* of Pacariqtambo have continued in existence as landholding groups and as the principal groups for the performance of public communal labor for the four and one-half centuries of the recorded history of the community. The historical documents from Pacariqtambo are replete with examples in which the *ayllus*, through their representative headmen, have waged a continuous struggle against such forces as the haciendas for the control of land and other resources within the district (e.g., A.M.A.C., exps.# 2073, 9288). Therefore, while space does not permit an exhaustive study of these issues and processes, it is nonetheless important to bear in mind that an understanding of these processes is fundamental to the historical analysis of the reproduction and transformation of sociopolitical groupings in Pacariqtambo since colonial times. These comments are directly related to the second point of clarification.

As I will utilize contemporary ethnographic data as a point of departure for the discussions in the next two chapters, I should clarify a few points concerning the use of ethnographic analogy in the project of comparing sociopolitical groups during different historical periods that I will undertake here. In the first place, we cannot assume, for instance, that what is referred to as an "*ayllu*" today is equivalent in every respect to what was identified by this term in the sixteenth century. *Ayllus* in Pacariqtambo today are residentially nonlocalized landholding groups whose members may or may not consider themselves related by close kinship ties. *Ayllu* members are responsible for undertaking public labor projects as a group and for celebrating communitywide religious festivals.

While the sixteenth-century *ayllus* of Pacariqtambo were also landholding and public labor groups, it is highly likely that at that time *ayllu* members were related by close kinship ties and that the *ayllus* were residentially localized. The latter would have been true both in the case of the pre-"reduction," dispersed *ayllus* and in the case of the pattern of residence of the *ayllu* members within the newly created reduction in the early 1570s; that is, at the time of their reduction, the *ayllus* were probably each assigned a sector within the village (see Spalding, 1984:214). Therefore, residential localization and degree of kinship relatedness are two specific features with respect to which the contemporary *ayllus* may differ significantly from their sixteenth-century counterparts.

These comments on the transformation of *ayllus* over the course of the past several centuries hold for other institutions (e.g., moieties) and practices as well. But beyond these comments on how such institutions as *ayllus* and moieties have changed over time, there is still a need to explain how and why *any* similarities or "continuities" in the composition of *ayllus*—such as those illustrated in the *ayllu* lists in table 4—might exist at all. Here, we should recognize that the problem of the use of ethnographic analogy in historical comparisons involves more complex issues than the evaluation of specific changes, for instance, in the modes of recruitment, residence patterns, and so on, of *ayllus* from the colonial period to the present. A larger issue concerns the ideological orientation that one takes in the historical analysis of colonized populations, particularly in such settings as the postconquest Andean world in which the historical record is almost exclusively the product of elites (both Spanish and native). The problem is one of the degree to which one imputes, and therefore is prepared to recognize, the attributes of willfullness and historical self-consciousness to such subordinate, colonized populations.

The historical record in the Andes from the colonial period to the present is replete with examples illustrating the often complete disregard, or subversion, of laws, institutions, and new forms of organization that were imposed over time by a variety of dominant outside forces, such as the state and the church. This is seen in the colonial period, for instance, in the continuation of elements of pre-Hispanic religious practices well beyond the time when the Spanish were confident that their efforts at proselytization had been successful (Acosta, 1987; Cock C. and Doyle, 1979; Flores Galindo, 1986; Rowe, 1957; Salomon, 1985; Stern, 1982*a*, 1982*b*; Wachtel, 1971); in the partial, or in some cases total, abandonment of the reductions soon after their creation (Gade and Escobar, 1982; Pease, 1977:109; Saignes, 1987; Spalding, 1984); and in the failure of attempts to disenfranchise local hereditary lineages of *caciques principales* from positions of authority in the colonial system of governance (Saignes, 1987; Spalding, 1984).

Such a record of the disregard, subversion, or "appropriation" of imposed institutions by the Andean peasantry from colonial times to the present calls for more than a passive or even cynical interpretation of such a record of relative continuity as that illustrated by the six lists of *ayllus* in Pacariqtambo recorded in table 4. Such a record, I would argue, is not the product merely of a persistence in nomenclature extending over four centuries, but rather is evidence of the willful and self-conscious manipulation of political groups and social categories by successive generations of residents of this community as a part of their local tactics of confrontation and accommodation with changing social, political, and economic circumstances (Urton, 1988). Viewed from this perspective, ethnographic analogy in the particular setting that we are discussing is grounded in an elaborate and well-formulated *local* theory and practice of social organization. It is from this perspective that I will explore the relevance of the contemporary ethnographic data for providing a theoretical orientation for interpreting the organization of *ayllus* and moieties in Pacariqtambo in the past.

An Ethnographic Description of Social and Territorial Groups in Pacariqtambo

The modern-day town of Pacariqtambo (plate 6) has a population of some 950 Quechua- and bilingual Quechua- /Spanish-speaking people whose livelihood is based primarily on agriculture and herding. The town was formally recognized as a *comunidad de indígenas* (native community) in 1946. Pacariqtambo is today the capital of a district of the same name in the Province of Paruro; the district was created in 1964 by executive order of the president of Peru at the time, Fernando Belaúnde Terry. There are some thirteen other villages within the district; six of these villages have traditionally been recognized as administrative "annexes" (*anexos*) of the central town (Urton, 1988).

To outline the central features of the organization of sociopolitical groups in the town and district of Pacariqtambo today, I will begin with a discussion of the *ayllus* and moieties of the central town itself and expand the description to show how the "peripheral" (annex) villages are incorporated into this nuclear organization (see map 3).

The Ayllus and Moieties of the Town of Pacariqtambo

The principal suprahousehold units of social, political, and ritual organization in Pacariqtambo are the *ayllus*. There are ten *ayllus* in the town (one additional *ayllu*—Qoipa—is located outside of town; see below). They are evenly divided into moieties, called Hanansayaq (of the upper part) and Hurinsayaq (of the lower part). The *ayllus* are listed in their respective moiety groupings in table 4, column 6. In modern-day Pacariqtambo, *ayllus* are composed of groups of individuals who may or may not have close kinship ties to one another. The *ayllus* are reproduced primarily in a patrilineal fashion. Children are considered to belong (in an informal sense) to the *ayllu* of their father. Upon marriage, a man will usually become a full, participating member in his father's *ayllu*; a woman will usually adopt the *ayllu* affiliation of her husband (Urton, 1985a, n.d.b).

The corporate basis for the *ayllus* is the joint ownership by all the *ayllu* members of parcels of land that traditionally have been considered to belong to these groups. Each *ayllu* member has usufruct and inheritance rights over one or more parcels of this land. For most day-to-day purposes, *ayllu* land is managed as though it were privately owned; however, *ayllu* members may not sell or otherwise alienate their parcels of land without the consent of the *ayllu* as a

Plate 6. Pacariqtambo

whole. It should also be noted in regard to their overall relationship to land that the *ayllus* are the units for the annual redistribution of the high-altitude communal potato lands (Kater, *n.d.,* 1988; Urton, 1988). Finally, *ayllu* members are jointly responsible for celebrating one communitywide festival—a Catholic saint's day—every year and for working together in communal work parties on different occasions during the year (Urton, 1984, 1986).

The status of the moieties in the organization of activities in the town is less easily defined than that of the *ayllus*. The principal settings in which the moiety groupings are reproduced today are on those occasions when all of the *ayllus* are called together to participate in public events, such as during community assemblies or work parties. On such occasions, it is common for the community officials to enumerate the *ayllus* (e.g., in assigning work tasks) in an order that begins with the first *ayllu* of the upper moiety, proceeds through the other four *ayllus* of that moiety, and ends with the five *ayllus* of the lower moiety. What is important to note about this order is that Hanansayaq is formally ranked above Hurinsayaq and that each moiety is ranked internally, from the first to the last (fifth) *ayllu*. These intermoiety rankings are based on distinctions among the *ayllus* in terms of size, conceived age, the relative burden demanded by the festivals they sponsor and other factors that we need not go into here (see Urton 1986, 1988).

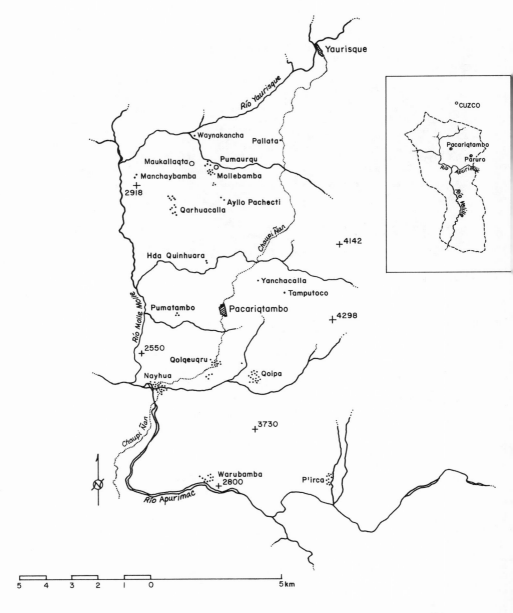

Map 3. The District of Pacariqtambo (clusters of dots indicate village settlements)

The relative "ages" of the *ayllus* are expressed most clearly in local ideas about their origins. That is, it is said by people in the town today that at the beginning of time, there were only two "*ayllus*" in Pacariqtambo: "Hanansayaq" and "Hurinsayaq." These two original *ayllus*—now the names of the moieties—expanded and became differentiated over time. The lowest, fifth-ranked groups—Qarhuacalla Segundo and Pumatambo—gained the status of *ayllus* only in this century (Urton, 1988).

The name and status of *ayllu Nayhua*—the first *ayllu* of the upper moiety (table 4)—provide keys to understanding the conceptual basis for ranking among the ten *ayllus* (not just among those of Hanansayaq). On virtually all occasions, Nayhua is the first group mentioned in enumerations of the *ayllus*. It is not uncommon to hear Nayhua referred to as "*qollana ayllu*" (first, supreme *ayllu*). The word *nayhua* appears to be a conflation of the Quechua term *mayhua* and the Aymara term *nayra*. Nayhua is the name of an *ayllu* in Pacariqtambo as well as a village to the southwest of Pacariqtambo, in the Apurimac River Valley (map 3). *Nayhua* is also the name of a colorful flower (*Stenomesson variegatum*) that grows in warm, subtropical climates; the flower grows in the annex village of Nayhua (it does not grow at the higher altitude of the town of Pacariqtambo). This flower is referred to in the literature as both *nayhua* and *mayhua* (Soukup, 1970: 327–329). In a document from 1571, Nayhua ayllu is called Naivapuca, "red flower" (Ulloa, 1909).

On the other hand, in Bertonio's early seventeenth-century dictionary of Aymara, *nayra* is given as a synonym for *collana* (*qollana*); both terms are glossed as "the first" (Bertonio, 1984 [1612]). Bertonio (1984 [1612]: 231–232) also gives the following glosses for *nayra*: *nayra pacha* (ancient); *nayraja* (without, or before, time); *nayra* (the tip, or beginning of something, such as a rope); *nayra* (eye, or eyes of the face); *nayra* (a seed of grain, such as maize, quinua, etc.). Bertonio also says that *nayra ppia* is synonymous with *ttokho*. The latter is the Aymara form of the Quechua term *t'oqo* (window), as found in the earlier references to the caves (or windows) of origin at Tampu T'oqo. Thus, *qollana/nayra/nayhua* is the window, or opening—the first in the series and the point of origin—of the *ayllus* of Pacariqtambo. The most common answer that I received to the question of why the *ayllus* of Hanansayaq are considered to be above (or "prior to") those of Hurinsayaq was that, since Nayhua ayllu is *qollana ayllu*, the upper moiety is *qollana* (first) as well. There is, then, a kind of "codetermination" between the first position in a ranked series and the hierarchical relationship between the two moieties into which the series is divided.

In addition to Nayhua, there is one other *ayllu* name in table 4, column 6, that indicates a particular position in a ranked series: Qarhuacalla. In Inka political classifications, *qarhua* (dry) referred to the fourth (ascending) position in a ranked series of five ancestors, and to the fourth position in a hierarchical system of five administrative officials (Zuidema, 1986:37, 39). In terms of its use in designating a position in a ranked series, *qarhua* may be related to the Quechua adverb *karu*, "far, distant." In González Holguín's early seventeenth-century dictionary of Quechua, he glosses *Caru runa* as "foreigner, stranger, one who comes from far away" (1952 [1608]:51). In hierarchical classifications containing four ranked positions, *karu* refers to the lowest, fourth, position; for example, relatives of the fourth degree (Zuidema, 1982c). *Calla* (or *cayao*) can be glossed as "origin, or base" (González Holguín, 1952 [1608]:61; Zuidema, 1982c). In a ranked series of three categories, *calla/cayao* is the last, third, position in the series. Therefore, *qarhuacalla* is the "distant, fourth degree" group, or category. Something beyond *"qarhuacalla"*—such as a fifth-ranking group—is "beyond the distant," near the margins with the outside.

Qarhuacalla has been ranked as the fourth *ayllu* of the upper moiety of Pacariqtambo since 1792. It will be recalled that in 1569, Qarhuacalla (Caruacalla) was said to have been the *ayllu* affiliation of Kilaku Yupanki Inka, the Inka-by-Privilege who was the great-grandfather of Rodrigo Sutiq Callapiña. At the beginning of this century, Qarhuacalla *ayllu* was split into two groups, producing Qarhuacalla Primero and Qarhuacalla Segundo; today, these two *ayllus* are the fourth and fifth *ayllus* of the upper moiety, respectively (Urton, 1988). Qarhuacalla Segundo replaced Pachecti as the fifth *ayllu* of the upper moiety. In the Inka origin myth, Pachecti (Pachete) was the name of the first place where the ancestors stopped after leaving Tampu T'oqo, on their way to Cuzco (see chap. 2).

These comments on the symbolic and classificatory implications of the words *nayhua* and *qarhuacalla* are relevant not only for understanding the organization and ranking of the ten *ayllus* in Pacariqtambo today, but for comparing the contemporary system with that of the ranking of nonroyal *ayllus* in Inka Cuzco as discussed earlier (e.g., the status of the fifth *ayllu* of the moieties of Cuzco—Sañuq and Oro/Uru—as distant, outside groups). In fact, Pacariqtambo is an exceptionally important community for study in relation to such problems because, while the population of the Cuzco Valley in Inka times was divided into ten royal and ten nonroyal *ayllus*, each set of which was divided between the two moieties, and while decimal organization was a pervasive feature of the administration of populations throughout the Inka empire (Julien, 1982), Pacariqtambo is to the best of my knowledge the only community in the circum-Cuzco region today where one finds an organization of ten *ayllus* divided into moieties.

I stated earlier that the fifth *ayllus* of the moieties in Pacariqtambo—Qarhuacalla Segundo and Pumatambo—are relatively "new" *ayllus*. In addition, many of the members of these two *ayllus* actually live outside the central town, in villages of the same names as the *ayllus* (map 3). Therefore, in terms of their residence patterns, the designation of the fifth *ayllus* as "beyond the distant" fourth degree is an accurate description of these two groups, which share certain characteristics with both the *ayllus* and the annex villages. I will return to a more thorough discussion of the intermediate position of the fifth *ayllus* after a description of the annexes.

The Formation of the Moiety System at the District Level

Six of the thirteen villages that are located within the district, around the central town of Pacariqtambo, are considered to be administrative annexes of the district capital. In 1988 the main difference between annex and nonannex villages was that the former had the responsibility for sending the images of their patron saints to participate in the principal festival in Pacariqtambo, the festival of the Virgin of the Nativity, celebrated on September 8. Members of the annexes also occasionally helped in communal work parties organized by the *ayllus* in Pacariqtambo; for instance, residents of the annexes helped repair the truck road that services Pacariqtambo. It is interesting to note that on these occasions, as well as in everyday conversations, the annex villages and their residents are often referred to as the *qatay* (sons-in-law) of the *ayllus* of Pacariqtambo (Urton, n.d.b).

Up until the time of the Agrarian Reform in the early 1970s, there existed more formal ties between Pacariqtambo and the annexes; these came about in the form of a system of dual (moiety-based) prestige hierarchies of officials called *varayuqkuna* (staff holders).[1] The *varayuqkuna* were political and ritual officials drawn from among the memberships of the *ayllus* and annexes who were responsible for the conduct of public affairs within the district. Each moiety had its respective hierarchy of officials; the activities of the two sets of *varayuqkuna* were coordinated by the governor and the *caciques,* or, in more recent times, by the president and the mayor (see Isbell, 1985; Skar, 1982). Each *ayllu* and annex within the two moieties had a set of three *varayuqkuna* officials; these included a

Table 5. *The Annexes of the Moieties*

Annexes of Hanansayaq	Annexes of Hurinsayaq
Nayhua	Qoipa
Qolqueuqru	P'irca
Mollebamba/Ayllo Pachecti	Warubamba

maestro vara (the head official) and two assistants, called *alguaciles* or *regidores*—the former served the *maestros varas* of the *ayllus*, the latter, those of the annexes. The *varayuqkuna* of three of the annexes, and therefore the annex villages themselves, belonged to Hanansayaq; the other three annexes belonged to Hurinsayaq (table 5).

One could say that through the organization of the prestige hierarchies, the moiety system of Pacariqtambo was extended to incorporate the population in the surrounding territory. However, it would be equally correct to say that the moiety system was a product of the interactions and hierarchical relations between the *ayllus* and the annexes. Therefore, the overall organization of politicoritual groups within the district of Pacariqtambo has traditionally been composed of four basic categories of social groups produced by the *intersection* of the distinction between Hanansayaq and Hurinsayaq, on the one hand, with that between the *ayllus* and the annexes, on the other (fig. 2).

It is important here to note that there has traditionally been a spatial dimension to the moiety division within the district. This is partially defined by the locations of the annexes of the moieties with respect to the route of the principal footpath that passes through the district, Chaupi Ñan (middle road). Chaupi Ñan runs through the district from the village of Nayhua, which is located to the southwest of Pacariqtambo, through the town of Pacariqtambo, and on to the northeast, passing through Pallata, and to Yaurisque. When we study the locations of the villages that are considered to belong to each moiety (table 5 and map 3), we find that the annexes of Hanansayaq are all located in the northwestern half of the district. The village associated with the fifth *ayllu* of the upper moiety (Qarhuacalla), is also located to the northwest. The annex villages of Hurinsayaq, on the other hand, are located in the southeastern half of the district, as defined by the footpath of Chaupi Ñan. However, the fifth *ayllu* village of the lower moiety, Pumatambo, is not located to the east of Pacariqtambo, as one might expect from the moiety division, but to the west. This is the one exception to the northwest/south-

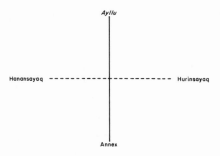

Fig. 2. The intersection of the moiety division and the division between the *ayllus* and the annexes

Table 6. *The Origin Places of the* Ayllus

Ayllu	Origin Place(s)
Hanansayaq	
Nayhua	Coralpata and Qolqueuqru
Quinhuara	Cerro Quinhuara Grande
Aqchakar	Cerro Aqchakar
Qarhuacalla	Qarhuacalla
Pachecti	Pachecti
Hurinsayaq	
San Miguel	Sullukllapata and Santa Maria
P'irca	Jurinka
Yanchacalla	Cerro Yanchacalla
Huaycho	Pukarapata
Qoipa	Qoipa
Pumatambo	Pumatambo

east division between Hanansayaq and Hurinsayaq.

The territorial division between the moieties is also reflected in people's opinions about the locations of the origin places of the ten *ayllus*. That is, each *ayllu* is considered to have originated at a specific place around the town of Pacariqtambo. These places, which are where the ancestors of the *ayllu* are considered actually to have lived and where the spirits of those ancestors (*machulas*, or *ñawpa machus*) live today, are all located on low hilltops or mountains within the district (Urton, 1984). The origin places of the *ayllus* are identified in table 6 and map 4. The concept of "*ayllu* origin places"

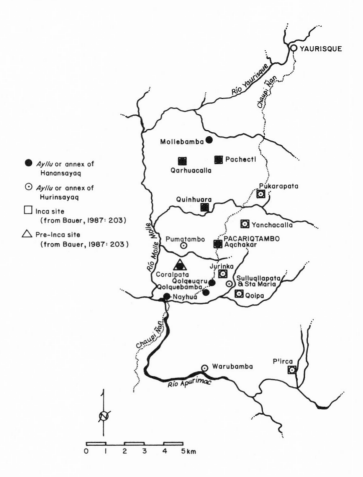

Map 4. *Ayllu* origin places and archaeological sites in Pacariqtambo

seems to represent contemporary thinking concerning the locations of the places from where the *ayllus* were reduced into the central town of Pacariqtambo in the late sixteenth century. This local theory finds some confirmation in the results of an archaeological survey of the district of Pacariqtambo that was carried out by Brian Bauer.

Bauer's survey identified fifteen pre-Hispanic habitation sites within the district (1987:202–203). Eight of the habitation sites that date from Inka times correspond to the traditional origin places of eight of the *ayllus*. Coralpata, the origin place of *ayllu* Nayhua—the first *ayllu* of the upper moiety—is associated with a *pre*-Inkaic site (map 4). It is also important to point out here that the origin places of the two *ayllus* that were classified as the fifth *ayllu* of the moieties until the present century—Pachecti and Yanchacalla (table 4, cols. 3–5)—were also identified in Bauer's survey as Inka-period sites. Pachecti, the old fifth *ayllu* of the upper moiety, and the first stopping place of the Inkas after leaving Tampu T'oqo, is located to the northwest of Chaupi Ñan; Yanchacalla, the old fifth *ayllu* of the lower moiety, is situated to the east of this foot trail. I will have more to say concerning the locations of the origin places of the *ayllus* in the overall territorial division between the moieties later in this chapter.

The Concentric Representation of Political and Residential Groups in Pacariqtambo

When we take into account both the territorial dimensions and the hierarchical rankings of the *ayllus* and annexes within the district of Pacariqtambo, we find that the political groupings and settlements defined by the dual divisions and quadripartite structure shown in figure 2 can be meaningfully grouped within the following concentric categories: (1) the "inside"; (2) the "border" (inside/outside); and (3) the "outside." I have discussed as thoroughly as is necessary here the inside and outside groups, which are composed, respectively, of the *ayllus* and annexes. However, there remain several points that should be made concerning the middle—or border—category of the concentric scheme outlined above. The border category is composed of those groups that share certain characteristics with both the *ayllus* and the annexes. It is important to elaborate on the concentric organization of relations among groups within the district because we will find in these data several points of interest for an interpretation of the sixteenth-century Inka origin narratives from the point of view of Pacariqtambo.

Concerning the border category in the concentric organization, it was established earlier that the two fifth *ayllus* of the moieties, Qarhuacalla Segundo and Pumatambo, which, like annexes, have residential bases outside the town of Pacariqtambo, mediate between the inside and outside groups in both geographical (i.e., residential) and classificatory terms. These two *ayllus* may therefore be included within a middle, border category of the concentric representation of social and territorial groups within the district.

Another member of the border category is *Qoipa*. Qoipa, which is one of the annex villages of the lower moiety (table 5), is located some 4 kilometers to the south of Pacariqtambo (maps 3 and 4). The village of Qoipa actually contains another, that is, the *eleventh*, *ayllu* of the District of Pacariqtambo. About twenty-five heads of household in this village of some four hundred people belong to an *ayllu* of Pacariqtambo called Qoipa *ayllu*. As we see in table 4, Qoipa is listed as an *ayllu* of the town of Pacariqtambo in historical documents from 1568 to 1836. The history of Qoipa *ayllu* is fascinating and complex, but unfortunately, we cannot go into that history at length here (see Urton, 1988). For the moment, it will suffice to have established that, like the two fifth *ayllus* of the moieties, Qoipa is a village in the district that incorporates within it an *ayllu* of the town of Pacariqtambo; therefore, Qoipa combines features of both the *ayllus* and the annexes.

A fourth member of the intermediate, border category is the village of Pachecti, which is located some 5 kilometers to the north of Pacariqtambo (maps 3 and 4). Pachecti (referred to today as Ayllo Pachecti) and the nearby village of Mollebamba make up the incorporated peasant community known officially as Mollebamba–Ayllo Pachecti (SINAMOS, 1976:97–98). Until the beginning of this century, Pachecti was the fifth *ayllu* of the upper moiety in Pacariqtambo (table 4; see Urton, 1984, 1988, n.d.b). The earliest reference that I am aware of to an *ayllu* Pachecti is from 1568 (Glave, personal communication; n. 3). Pachecti lost its status as an *ayllu* sometime between 1910 and 1930. The reason for this appears to have been primarily demographic; that is, throughout the nineteenth century, *ayllu* Pachecti was composed of only one or two members. In addition, the lands of Pachecti were taken over by an hacienda at the beginning of this century.[2] Pachecti was replaced as the fifth *ayllu* of Hanansayaq by Qarhuacalla Segundo (table 4). Thus, despite the fact that Pachecti is not today an *ayllu*, it did have that status throughout most of the recorded history of Pacariqtambo. Pachecti has therefore traditionally constituted a member of the intermediate category of settlements within the district.

Figure 3 is a diagram summarizing the concentric representation of social and territorial groups within the district of Pacariqtambo as described in the foregoing discussion. The diagram shows the opposition between the *ayllus* inside Pacariqtambo and the annex villages outside *mediated* by the four "*ayllu*-settlements" just described. Three of the four villages that are included in the border category—Qarhuacalla Segundo, Qoipa, and Pumatambo—have a complicated, intermediary status in the organization of sociopolitical and territorial groups within the district today. That is, with the

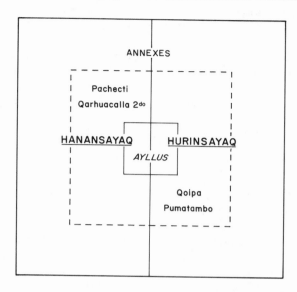

Fig. 3. The concentric representation of sociopolitical groups and settlements in Pacariqtambo

exception of Pachecti, these groups are typical *ayllus* in the sense that they all own *ayllu* land, celebrate communitywide festivals in the town of Pacariqtambo, participate in communal work parties, and so on, yet, like annexes, they have residential bases outside Pacariqtambo.

What is important to recognize for our purposes here is that from the latter part of the eighteenth century—by which time the moiety organization, as well as the ranking of the *ayllus*, becomes clear in the historical documents (see table 4 and below)—until the beginning of this century, Pachecti was also in this intermediate category of social and territorial groups in Pacariqtambo. One of my arguments in the conclusions will be that Pachecti and other nearby settlements (e.g., Waynakancha and Pallata) in the north of the district, which have traditionally belonged to the upper moiety of Pacariqtambo, may be classified as border communities in the organization of groups within the district. As such, Pachecti and these neighboring settlements were, *from the point of view of the central, collective focus of* ayllu *organization in Pacariqtambo,* in an appropriately "marginal" geographical location and they had a sufficiently ambiguous social classification, for representation by local people in the sixteenth century, as places associated with the origin of the Inka

ancestors. The latter were, again, from the point of view of Pacariqtambo, royal "outsiders."

With these descriptions of the contemporary social, political, and
territorial organizations in the town and district of Pacariqtambo as
background, we can now turn to a discussion of the organization of
social groups in this area in early colonial times.

An Introduction to the Distribution of the *Ayllus* before the Reduction

What was the nature of the organization of *ayllus* in the area of
Pacariqtambo before, and soon after, their reduction into a "new
town" in 1571? We have already encountered references in the material from 1569 in the Callapiña Document to two of the *ayllus* of
Pacariqtambo (Anchacari and Caruacalla) before the time of their reduction into a nucleated community. Anchacari (Aqchakar) was the
ayllu affiliation of Rodrigo Sutiq Callapiña; Caruacalla (Qarhuacalla)
was the *ayllu* of Kilaku Yupanki Inka. These were just two of eleven
dispersed *ayllus,* or what are referred to in one document from 1568
as *pueblos* (towns; it is unclear whether these were actual nucleated
settlements or *ayllus* dispersed over a limited area), in this area before the reduction.

The document from 1568 is a petition drawn up by the headmen
(*principales*) of the eleven *ayllus* that made up the *repartimiento*
of Pacariqtambo. They were requesting the removal, for certain un-
disclosed offenses, of the *cacique principal* at that time, don Alonso
Cauncho, and his replacement by Pedro Calla Piña (Callapiña). The
names of all eleven of the headmen are given in this document,
but only six of the *ayllus* are identified by name: Pachicti, Caruacalla, Quinuara, Acchacara, Cuño, and Cuypa (Glave, personal
communication).[3]

What is of immediate interest in this list for a consideration of the
origin myth is that it identifies one of the prereduction, dispersed
ayllus of Pacariqtambo as Pachicti (*Pachete, Pachecti*). In the versions of the Inka origin myth recorded by Cabello Valboa and Murúa,
Pachecti was said to have been the first place where the Inkas stopped
after leaving Tampu T'oqo; it was here that Manqo Qhapaq and
Mama Oqllu conceived a child (Sinchi Ruq'a), who would later succeed Manqo Qhapaq as the second king of the empire.

Although the toponym Pachete probably had little significance for
Cabello Valboa and Murúa, to anyone familiar with the political geography of the area of Pacariqtambo, mention of this place would
have brought to mind the following points: Pachecti was located just

above (i.e., to the south of) Pumaurqu, the site that may have been recognized by the Inkas as Tampu T'oqo; Pachecti overlooked the Yaurisque River, the actual geographical boundary between Pacariqtambo and the Cuzco Valley; and Pachecti was an *ayllu* of the upper moiety of Pacariqtambo. I will elaborate on these and other features of the status of Pachecti as we proceed.

In 1571, the eleven dispersed *ayllus* of the *repartimiento* of Pacariqtambo were reduced into the nucleated village of San Pedro de Quiñoca (Ulloa, 1909). The eleven *ayllus* are identified in table 4, column 2. The eleven pre- and early postreduction *ayllus* composed the *encomienda*, or *repartimiento* (i.e., a nonterritorial grant of patronage over a group of Indians) called Paccarictambo. The holder of the *encomienda* grant was Luis Palomino (Toledo 1975 [1583]: 151). The *ayllus* that made up this *encomienda* appear to have belonged to the Maskas ethnic group, although not all of the Maskas were included within this one *encomienda* (Toledo, 1975 [1583]: 151; Poole, 1984).

It is likely that the territory from which the eleven *ayllus* were drawn approximately coincided with the area included within the boundaries of the district of Pacariqtambo today (map 3). This was probably the case because, first, the district contains well-defined geographical boundaries on all four sides of what is essentially a rectangular area; these boundaries include the Yaurisque, Molle Molle and Apurimac rivers on the north, west, and south, and a zone of high (forty-two hundred to forty-three hundred meters) tundra or *puna* land to the east. Second, in the earliest description that we have of the lands of the *ayllus* (a document from 1595, see below), these lands are all located within the boundaries of the present-day district of Pacariqtambo. This is not to say that the *ayllus* did not have lands elsewhere, nor that *ayllus* and ethnic groups centered outside this area did not have lands within the "traditional" boundaries of the reduction of Pacariqtambo, but rather that this was probably the home territory of the *ayllus* that were reduced into this town.

We do not know exactly when the settlement that was reduced in 1571 under the name San Pedro de Quiñoca came to be known by the name of the *encomienda* grant of Indians who lived within the town, *Pacariqtambo* (Paccarictambo). As we will see in a moment, the town is explicitly referred to as Paccarictambo in a document dating to 1595. In documents from 1643 and 1714, the Inkaic ruins that are known today as Maukallaqta are almost certainly identified as "el pueblo viejo de Paccarictambo" (the old town of Pacariqtambo; A.M.A.C. exp. #17733, 34v).

It was suggested in chapter 2 that the site of Maukallaqta was probably originally known as Pacariqtambo and that sometime during the first few decades after the founding of the reduction of San Pedro de Quiñoca the name "Pacariqtambo" was transferred to this new town. It is now possible to document—in a way that will be meaningful in relation to the geographical configuration of *ayllu* origin places and settlements within the region of Pacariqtambo—why it seems to be the case that Maukallaqta was originally known as Pacariqtambo.

I give below translations of two passages from documents concerning land titles in the northern part of the territory controlled by Pacariqtambo during the seventeenth and eighteenth centuries. The first passage, which dates to 1643, is from a document included in the collection at present held by the Coronel family in Pacariqtambo. This document pertains to the assignment of land in the area of Manchaybamba to a man from Paruro named Pasqual Quispicapi. (Manchaybamba is located in the Molle Molle River Valley, just to the west of the village annex of Qarhuacalla and to the southwest of Maukallaqta; see map 3). It is intriguing to note in passing that Pasqual Quispicapi, who was the "Casique Principal" of Paruro at this time, was married to a woman from Pacariqtambo named María Magdalena; María—who is referred to in the document as "Tambo ñusta" ([Pacariq-] Tambo princess)—was the niece of Rodrigo Sutiq Callapiña (Rodrigo was her father's brother). "This same day, month and year [26 November 1643], I [the land judge] went to the place of Ynquelbamba and Manchaybamba, placing in possession of the said don Pasqual Quispicapi . . . eight *topos* [a land measure] in the place Albiray, bordering on the lands of don Juan Rauraua and on the other side with Chuchipiray and on the upper side with *a mountain called Biracochay* [Wiraqocha] and on the lower side with the lands of Pedro Gamarra" (my emphasis).[4]

The next passage, which comes from a document dating to 1714, concerns the delineation of the boundaries of the lands of an hacienda in the area between Mollebamba and Qarhuacalla (see map 3): "In the places of Mollebamba and other names there were measured the lands of the said hacienda bordering on one side with lands of Pedro Gamarra which are separated from each other by a valley called Guaman Uras Guaycco, which goes up to the river that comes down from Yaurisque, and along the upper part of the said valley up to *the mountain called Viracocha-urcco* water flows from *the old town of Pacariqtambo*" (A.M.A.C., exp. #17733 : 34v; my emphasis).[5]

Therefore, the "old town of Paccarictambo" was located on a mountain called Wiraqocha, or Viracocha-urcco (Wiraqocha mountain), which was in the area between Manchaybamba and Mollebamba (map 3). The second passage cited gives a fairly accurate picture of the disposition of river valleys and the direction of the flow of water in the immediate environs of the ruins of Maukallaqta. Without going into a detailed topographical analysis, I can affirm from my own knowledge of the area in question that the above passages provide reasonably convincing proof that, at least in the view of local people in the seventeenth and early eighteenth centuries, the Inka ruins of Maukallaqta were originally known as the "old town of Paccarictambo."

We should pause briefly here to consider the location of the place where the new town of Pacariqtambo was built (i.e., the *reducción*). In map 4, we see that the *ayllus* were brought together into a town that was located approximately at the mountain that is identified today as the traditional place of origin of ayllu Aqchakar. It will be recalled that Aqchakar (Anchacari) was the *ayllu* with which Rodrigo Sutiq Callapiña was affiliated. I would suggest that perhaps as a consequence of his successful accounting to the Spanish in 1569 of the noble ancestry of his lineage, Rodrigo may have had a privileged voice two years later in helping the Spanish decide where to build the new town of Pacariqtambo.

If this hypothesis is correct, then Rodrigo Sutiq Callapiña may have played an even more influential and direct role in the "localization," or concretization, of Pacariqtambo than was suggested earlier in connection with the legal proceeding in which he established his descent from Manqo Qhapaq. That is, Rodrigo Sutiq Callapiña could have been responsible for the relocation of all of the local *ayllus* from their various places of residence to the home territory of his (i.e., Rodrigo's) *own ayllu*, Aqchakar. As the place name Pacariqtambo became of increasing political significance not only to the local people, but also to the Spanish in Cuzco, the name was apparently adopted by the congeries of *ayllus* that had been brought together into the reduction called San Pedro de Quiñoca.

The first clear reference to the new town as "Pacariqtambo" appears in a document from 1595. The document is a *composición de tierras* (a record of the assigning of lands to the *ayllus* after their reduction) that was carried out by Francisco Alderrete Maldonado and Alonso Maldonado de Torres in 1594. This document is included in the private collection of the Coronel family; extracts from the document were copied into the petition that was drawn up in 1944 for the recognition of Pacariqtambo as an official *comunidad indígena* (A.M.A.C., #5877 : 12–14v). Interestingly, the man who is identified as the *cacique principal* in 1595 was named Pedro Agustín Callapiña. We cannot say for certain whether or not, and if so how, this man was related to Rodrigo Sutiq Callapiña. I suspect, however, that they *were* related, and that Pedro was the most recent descendant of what was a particularly long-lived—and undoubtedly hereditary—line of *caciques principales* in Pacariqtambo.

The document from 1595 is of particular interest in reconstructing the prereduction territorial organization of *ayllus* within the *repartimiento* of Pacariqtambo for three reasons. First, the document mentions two *pueblos viejos* (old towns) named Quinuara and San Miguel. While Quinuara is mentioned as an *ayllu* in the documents from 1568 and 1571, San Miguel is not mentioned in either of these earlier documents. We do not know, in fact, how San Miguel Ayllu may be related to any one of the *ayllus* that are mentioned in 1568 and 1571. San Miguel is today, as it has been since the late eighteenth century, the first *ayllu* of the lower moiety. It is said today that San Miguel had two places of origin: Sullukllapata and Santa María (map 4 and table 6). It is possible that one or the other (if not both) of the two *ayllus* that appear in the 1571 *ayllu* list in table 4, column 2, but that do *not* appear in the 1595 list in column 3—that is Cuño and Guatupasta—was renamed San Miguel at this time.

The significance of the reference to the "old towns" of Quinuara and San Miguel can best be clarified in relation to the second point of interest in the document from 1595. This concerns the status of the road that passed through the territory of Pacariqtambo at that time. The principal road through the territory is referred to in 1595 both as "the royal road [*camino real*] from Cuzco," and as "the royal road that comes from Chumbivilcas" (A.M.A.C., exp. #5877:13–14). Chumbivilcas is located to the south of Pacariqtambo, across the Apurimac River. In a document in the Coronel collection dating to 1643 (discussed earlier), the royal road that passed through the area of Pacariqtambo was described as follows: "*El camino rreal que biene del Valle de nayua camino de los Condesuyus que ba a la ciudad del Cuzco*" ("the royal road that comes from the Valley of Nayhua; the road of the Condesuyus [Kuntisuyus] that goes to the city of Cuzco"). The "Valley of Nayhua" refers to the Apurimac River Valley; the reference to Kuntisuyu is to the southern quadrant of the Inka empire.

The main footpath through the district of Pacariqtambo today is called Chaupi Ñan (middle road; maps 3 and 4). This footpath, which runs from the annex village of Nayhua (in the southwest), through Pacariqtambo and on to Pallata and Yaurisque (in the northeast), contains stretches of cobblestone paving. It can with reasonable certainty, I think, be identified with the royal road that went from Chumbivilcas, through Pacariqtambo, and on to Cuzco from 1595 to

1643. This royal road was one of the principal routes between Cuzco and populations to the south, that is, in Kuntisuyu, in Inka times. This brings us to the third point of interest in the 1595 document. I hypothesize that in the sixteenth century, the royal road through Pacariqtambo divided the prereduction, dispersed *ayllus* into moieties, just as Chaupi Ñan today divides the origin places of the *ayllus* into moieties. There are references in the 1595 *composición de tierras* that make it clear that the royal road through Pacariqtambo served as a boundary for the lands of *ayllus* of both the upper and lower moieties.[6] If the royal road to Cuzco in pre-Hispanic times and Chaupi Ñan today are, in fact, the same road, then the two "old towns" of Quinuara and San Miguel, which have been in different moieties since at least the early eighteenth century and which are located on opposite sides of Chaupi Ñan, may have served as "ritual centers" for their respective moieties before the time of the reduction.

Although we cannot say for certain, the original name of the present-day town of Pacariqtambo—San Pedro de Quiñoca—may have been taken from Quinhuara, the name of the traditional second *ayllu* of Hanansayaq and, perhaps, the ritual center for the *ayllus* of the upper moiety (San Pedro is the patron saint of the town; see chapter 5).

Summary: A Prelude to the Interpretation of the Inka Origin Myth

If we do accept the foregoing arguments and hypotheses, then we arrive at a point from which to interpret the toponyms mentioned in the early part of the legendary journey of the Inka ancestors from Tampu T'oqo to Cuzco in a way that has considerable geopolitical significance from the point of view of Pacariqtambo. That is, all of the places that are mentioned on the route of the legendary journey of the ancestors from Tampu T'oqo up to Pallata are located within the *upper moiety* of Pacariqtambo. After the ancestors left Pallata, they arrived at Haysquisrro. I have suggested that the toponym Haysquisrro may have referred to the town of Yaurisque, and that Yaurisque was just beyond the boundary of the lands controlled by the *ayllus* of Pacariqtambo. Therefore, the journey of the ancestors took them from within the territory of the upper moiety of Pacariqtambo up to the point that represented the boundary between the moieties, Chaupi Ñan (i.e., the royal road to Cuzco) and Pallata; the ancestors then passed along Chaupi Ñan outside of the territory of Pacariqtambo in their journey from Pallata to Yaurisque (Haysquisrro).

It is relevant to note here that Pallata was, in fact, considered to have been at, or near, the boundary between Pacariqtambo and Yaurisque in early colonial times. In a 1659 document in the Coronel collection that concerns the sale of land at Pallata, we find that Pallata is described as being located "en términos de los pueblos de yaurisque y pacaritambo" ("at the borders of the towns of Yaurisque and Pacariqtambo").[7]

An additional comment connecting the foregoing observations and earlier discussions of the origin places of the Inka ancestors and of the *ayllu* of Pacariqtambo is in order here. In chapter 2, it was pointed out that there are now two places within the District of Pacariqtambo that are identified as the Tampu T'oqo of the Inka origin myth; Tamputoco and Pumaurqu. Tamputoco is located to the northeast of Pacariqtambo, near the origin place of *ayllu* Yanchacalla (maps 2 and 4). Yanchacalla is at present the third *ayllu* of the lower moiety; however, as can be seen in table 4, Yanchacalla was the *fifth* *ayllu* of the lower moiety for most of the recorded history of the community. Pumaurqu, the other place of origin, is located within the territory of the incorporated community of Mollebamba–Ayllo Pachecti (maps 2 and 4). Until recent times, Pachecti was the *fifth* *ayllu* of the upper moiety. Therefore, the two sites identified today as Tampu T'oqo are located within different moieties, and they are near two sites that are identified as the origin places of *ayllus* that traditionally were ranked as border groups (i.e., fifth *ayllus*). From the point of view of the *ayllus* of Pacariqtambo, the two local origin places of the Inkas—the autochthonous inhabitants and original rulers of their land—were "near the borders with the outside" with respect to the hierarchical ranking and territorial organization of the *ayllus* and moieties in Pacariqtambo.

On the basis of the observations and hypotheses presented in this chapter, I would give the following interpretation of the Inka origin myth as seen from the perspective of the geopolitical organization of *ayllus* in the area of Pacariqtambo and between Pacariqtambo and Yaurisque. From the point of view of Pacariqtambo, the early part of the journey of the ancestors from Tampu T'oqo to Cuzco, in which the ancestors traveled through villages in the northern part of the territory of Pacariqtambo, was a narrative recapitulation of the moiety organization within Pacariqtambo and of its relationship to neighboring *ayllus* and ethnic groups. At the core of this narrative was a metaphorical comparison in which movement from the territory of Hanansayaq up to its border with Hurinsayaq (i.e., the movement from Tampu T'oqo and Pachecti to Pallata and Chaupi Ñan) *within* Pacariqtambo was likened to the movement from Pacariqtambo to one of its borders with the *outside*; in this case, Yaurisque occupied the position of the outside. In short, the origin myth is concerned with identifying boundaries within and between the territories of different ethnic groups from Pacariqtambo to Cuzco. I will elaborate on this interpretation of the origin myth in the conclusions.

In the next chapter I will discuss certain ritual practices within the district of Pacariqtambo today whereby the structures and principles of social and territorial organization described earlier are represented and reproduced. The specific rituals that I will discuss involve interactions among social groups within the district and between Pacariqtambo and the outside.

5. The Rituals and Ritual History of Divine Births and Boundaries

Introduction

The social and territorial groupings described in chapter 4 are the principal formal structures of the sociopolitical organization within the district of Pacariqtambo as identified today and as described in historical documents from the early colonial period. What is lacking now is an understanding of how people in the town and district of Pacariqtambo act on these formal structures to produce a "community." In the context of this study, to fail to move from the level of a formal description of the structures of society to a consideration of behavior within, and action on, those structures would be equivalent to describing the individuals and groups that appeared at the time of the emergence of the ancestors at Tampu T'oqo but failing to give an account of their journey to the valley of Cuzco. The social categories and groupings described in the Inka origin myth took on meaning only when they were set in motion along the route from Tampu T'oqo to Cuzco and began to interact among themselves and with other, outside groups. Similarly, it is through action—in the form of work, speech, ritual practice, and so on—that the social groupings, hierarchical relations, and other formal features of the organization of Pacariqtambo today take on meaning.

I will focus here on three ritual practices, all of which involve pilgrimages, or ritual circuits, that take place every year within the district of Pacariqtambo or between Pacariqtambo and its neighbors. These ritual pilgrimages are important for our study because they show how, through ritual practices, the *ayllus* and annex villages of Pacariqtambo today are integrated into a single, districtwide community and because they should provide a general understanding of the nature of interactions between Pacariqtambo and the outside—especially the town of Yaurisque—in ritual, political, economic, and other modes as well. With regard to the last point, it is important to stress that, although the rituals to be discussed in this chapter are all postconquest in their timing and overt symbolism, as they all celebrate Catholic saint's day festivals and other holy days in the Catholic calendar, similar types of interactions and ritual exchanges no doubt have a long history among populations within the area of Pacariqtambo, extending back into the colonial and pre-Hispanic eras. I would argue that a study of contemporary ritual interactions between Pacariqtambo and its neighbors may provide us with one avenue for investigating the history of politicoritual networks of interaction in this region in earlier times.

In more concrete terms, I will suggest here that the data to be discussed in this chapter on ritual pilgrimages may allow us to reflect in a meaningful way on certain crucial problems that arise from events and structures described in the Inka origin myth as described by residents of Pacariqtambo and Cuzco in the sixteenth and seventeenth centuries. The specific problems that I will be concerned with here include the following. First, what is the political significance, as seen from the point of view of geopolitical relations within Pacariqtambo, of the emergence of the ancestors from Tampu T'oqo and the subsequent conception and birth of the first child of the Inkas (Sinchi Ruq'a) in the area of Pachecti and Waynakancha? And second, what is the relevance of long-term patterns of pilgrimages and ritual circuits in the circum-Pacariqtambo area for an interpretation not only of these events, but of the journey of the ancestors from Pacariqtambo and Tampu T'oqo to Pallata, Yaurisque, and Cuzco? These are the central questions that motivate the study of rituals in this chapter.

The Nature and Significance of Continuities in Andean Ritual Practices

Despite the obvious interest and importance of the relationship between pre- and postconquest ritual traditions and interaction spheres alluded to earlier, we have, in fact, no thorough studies of the transformation of Andean rituals, much less of the evolution of ritual calendars in specific communities, during the first half-century following the Spanish conquest. In general, however, it is clear that traditional Andean religious beliefs and practices were not replaced wholly by European Catholic ones, but rather that the two traditions were integrated in the more subtle process referred to as "syncretism." In this process, the Andean religious rituals often continued to be practiced, but they were recast and reinterpreted in the new contexts and religious idioms supplied by Roman Catholicism (see Cock C. and Doyle, 1979; Flores Galindo, 1987; Wachtel, 1971). For instance, such a process probably occurred in the case of the celebration of the day of Cruz Velakuy, on May 3. This Catholic festival, which celebrates the Finding (*inventio*) of the Holy Cross, falls at the beginning of the harvest in the Andes. In many Andean communities, the crosses that belong to the community are fêted and mourned in all-night vigils that continue for two or three nights. Huertas Vallejos has shown that in northern Peru in early colonial and probably pre-Hispanic times, at the time of the harvest festival (K'arwa Mit'a) people stayed awake all night in wakes, called *Paqarikuy* (Huertas Vallejos, 1981:52; cf. Randall, *n.d.*:36). Therefore, in the case of Cruz Velakuy, the pre-Hispanic ritual was syncretized with, and incorporated by, the Catholic ritual.

It is important to stress that while syncretism provided the means whereby native, pre-Hispanic religious beliefs and practices continued to be observed in Andean communities into the colonial era, the traditional practices were nonetheless transformed as they were reproduced and reinterpreted in the new idioms, images, and ritual structures presented by Roman Catholicism. Syncretism was a process of negotiation in which both sides in the equation—the pre-Hispanic practices as well as the Spanish Catholic ones—underwent a transformation.

The fact that such transformations have taken place in Andean rituals over the centuries of course makes it difficult now to construct an interpretation of these practices that may have some relevance for the possible motivations that lay behind, and gave significance to, these practices in earlier times. An example of the type of situation that I am referring to here would be one in which, for instance, traditional (i.e., pre-Hispanic) exchanges and interactions between *ayllus* or ethnic groups within a certain region—through reciprocal feasting, ritual battles, and the like—became transformed in postconquest times into annual pilgrimages and reciprocal visitations between the Catholic saints that these groups (or villages) adopted as their patron saints (for an excellent discussion of such transformations in the circum-Cuzco region, see Sallnow, 1987:55–63, 268–269).

It is undoubtedly the case that in many such instances, it is no longer possible to disentangle the practices of today, carried out in their clearly expressed idioms of Roman Catholic symbolism and ritualism, from their original form(s). On the other hand, there were undoubtedly certain elements in the process of negotiation entailed in syncretism that may *not* have been radically transformed during the retranslation of patterns of interaction from one set of motivations, idioms, and their sponsoring images to another. For instance, there were a number of aspects of the performance of Catholic rituals in Andean communities that would not have been of particular interest or concern to the clergymen who oversaw, and officiated at, these festivals in early colonial times. For example, although the clergy within the newly formed reductions in the 1570s were concerned that certain festivals should be celebrated at the appropriate times during the year (e.g., Corpus Christi, Easter, Christmas, and a number of Marian festivals; see Poole, 1984:350–351, n. 9), there is no evidence that the clergymen concerned themselves with *which* particular individual, *ayllu*, or moiety within the community sponsored which festival.

When we find, as we will in the case of Pacariqtambo, that each *ayllu* in the community has—as they did in colonial times (e.g., Villanueva Urteaga, 1982:468)—the responsibility for sponsoring a particular saint's day festival, this undoubtedly represents an element of the ritual practice that was determined primarily on the basis of local political, economic, and social considerations, rather than reflecting a feature of the ritual calendar that was imposed (or controlled) by the clergymen who oversaw these ritual events in the past. Therefore, I would propose that, at least in the case of Pacariqtambo, the sponsorship of a particular Catholic saint's day festival by a particular *ayllu* reflects directly on the larger process of the negotiation of relations among the *ayllus* within the community as a whole. It is in this way that the analysis of rituals can provide a productive basis for developing hypotheses concerning the history of social, economic, and political organizations within a community.

There is one other factor that must be taken into account in the formula for relating ritual structure and sociopolitical organization outlined above. This concerns the role of the haciendas in the sponsorship of festivals beginning as early as the seventeenth century. As is true regarding the role of the haciendas in many other areas of life in Pacariqtambo (as elsewhere in the Andes), the role of these entities in the evolution of ritual calendars in the district is complex and not well attested in the available documentary materials. However, from comparative studies of this problem in the circum-Cuzco region, it is clear that the haciendas affected local ritual calendars in at least two ways. First, hacienda owners (*hacendados*) were able over time to exert increasing control over the management of the *cargo* systems through which festival sponsorship in the native communities was organized. This resulted in the enrichment of the cults of particular saints (often at the expense of others); tensions often arose between the *hacendados* and the natives over the management of the festivals and the control of the resources (e.g., land and labor) that were normally devoted to the care and maintenance of the saints (see Poole, 1984:116).

Second, it was common practice from the beginnings of the hacienda system for individual *hacendados* to sponsor their own saint's day celebrations. In many cases, these festivals conflicted, or were in competition, with those of the native communities (Poole, 1984:116). In addition, as Sallnow has demonstrated, especially in the case of hacienda festival sponsorship during the early colonial (as opposed to the later republican period), the sponsorship of festivals by the haciendas often resulted in conflicts between *hacendados* and the local ecclesiastical officials. "The institutionalization and legitimation of the new [colonial] estates within a rural social order dominated by doctrinas and state-controlled corregimientos was achieved largely through religious means. The very recognition of an hacienda as a center of population turned on whether or not it possessed a place of worship. . . . The establishment of de facto religious jurisdiction by an estate often met with fierce resistence [sic] from local clergy in the doctrinas" (Sallnow, 1987:171).

The clergy often resisted *hacendado* attempts to become involved in festival sponsorship because this represented one of the means whereby the *hacendados* were able to exercise control over the labor service (*mit'a*), which the Indians were required to perform under the rubric of devotion to the saints. The use and control of this labor service were ordinarily the prerogatives of the clergy (Sallnow, 1987:171).

For these reasons, an understanding of the full implications of the historical relationships between ritual calendars and sociopolitical organizations—at least in the circum-Cuzco region—must take into account the increasing influence that the haciendas exerted in these structures and practices. Later in this chapter, we will examine an hacienda-sponsored festival celebrated in the district of Pacariqtambo that exhibits some of the characteristics of hacienda festival sponsorship outlined above. This festival also represents a crucial component in the cycle of rituals, which, I will argue, have their earliest expressions in the accounts of the origin of the Inkas at Pacariqtambo/Tampu T'oqo.

The following discussion of three contemporary rituals in Pacariqtambo will provide the materials for elaborating my methodological and theoretical orientations in a way that will be relevant for interpreting the significance of the Inka origin myth for people in this area from the latter part of the sixteenth to the early eighteenth century. We will be concerned with, first, the significance for these people of accounts of the birth of divine beings (i.e., the ancestors of the Inkas) within their territory and the subsequent movement of these beings from Pacariqtambo, through Yaurisque, to Cuzco; and second, how people in Pacariqtambo used these accounts in their appropriations of Catholic ritualism as a part of their strategy for constructing and reproducing their own versions and theories of history.

The Ritual Integration of Pacariqtambo with the Outside: The Annual Visitations between San Pedro and San Esteban

One of the most important local pilgrimages that people in Pacariqtambo participate in today involves reciprocal visits between the statue, or "image" (*imagen*), of San Pedro, the patron saint of Pacariqtambo, and that of San Esteban, the patron saint of the town of Yaurisque. San Pedro has been identified as the patron saint of Pacariqtambo since the time of the reduction of the eleven *ayllus* into a single community in 1571 (recall that the town was originally called San Pedro de Quiñoca). People in Pacariqtambo and Yaurisque today agree that San Pedro and San Esteban are "brothers."

The visits between these two saints take place as follows. On August 8, the day of the celebration of the festival of San Esteban in the Catholic calendar, the statue of San Pedro is carried on a litter from Pacariqtambo, along Chaupi Ñan (through Pallata) to Yaurisque, where it remains for one week. The reciprocal visit by San Esteban to Pacariqtambo does not, interestingly enough, take place on the day of San Pedro in the calendar of Catholic saint's days (i.e., June 29); rather, this visit occurs on the day of the Virgin of the Nativity, September 8.

The celebration of the day of the Virgin of the Nativity in Pacariqtambo is the principal saint's day festival within the district. All of the saints' images housed in the church in Pacariqtambo are paraded around the central plaza on two or three occasions during the festival (plate 7). The Virgin of the Nativity—an eight-day festival—is the *cargo* responsibility of ayllu Nayhua, the first *ayllu* of the upper moiety (Urton, 1984, 1986). An important point to bear in mind concerning the timing of the reciprocal visits between San Pedro and San Esteban is that the period covered by these visits—August 8 to September 8—coincides with the beginning of the planting season.

In addition to the visit by San Esteban to Pacariqtambo, which takes place at the time of the feast of the Virgin of the Nativity, the six traditional annexes of Pacariqtambo send the statues of their patron saints into town on litters. The ritual duty of carrying them

Plate 7. Procession of the Virgin of the Nativity

Plate 8. Bearers of the image of Santiago from P'irqa. Photo by Jean-Jacques Decoster

to town and back is undertaken by *cargo* holders from the annexes; each musters support for this undertaking from friends, relatives, and *compadres* (ritual coparents). In many cases, the people who carry the saint (as well as the entourage that accompanies them) actually *run* all the way from the annex village to Pacariqtambo, stopping at certain well known places along the way to rest, pray to the saint, and drink *chicha* (corn beer). Plate 8 shows a rest stop by the group of people from the annex village of P'irca who were carrying their patron saint, Santiago, to Pacariqtambo in 1987.[1]

The visiting saints remain in Pacariqtambo for the duration of the festival of the Virgin of the Nativity, returning to their respective communities on the eighth day. Therefore, at the time of the festival of the Virgin of the Nativity, all of the saints' images in the church in Pacariqtambo, as well as those from the annexes, meet with a saint from the "outside"—San Esteban from Yaurisque.

The festival of the Virgin of the Nativity represents one of the principal settings in which the relations among the *ayllus* and annexes of Pacariqtambo are reaffirmed and reconstituted every year at the beginning of a new agricultural season. The presence of the outside saint is, I think, crucial for the reinforcement of relations among groups within the district at this time. San Esteban represents the (probably "elder") brother of San Pedro with respect to whom the various social, political, and ritual groups within the district annually reconstitute themselves as a unity (see Poole, 1984:300–302 for a similar interpretation of the significance of the festival of the Virgin of the Nativity in Paruro).

I think that it is particularly significant that this "reconstitution of the community," which takes place during the festival of the Virgin of the Nativity, occurs every year at the beginning of the agricultural season. As Poole has noted (1984:306), the Virgin of the Nativity has an especially important relationship to agricultural fertility and reproduction in general: "Even within the official Catholic liturgy, the Virgin, and especially the Virgin of the Nativity who gives birth to the son of God on earth, is represented as an 'earthly paradise,' a paradise emerging from the natural, human, and exclusively female fertility which she embodies. . . . In the Andes . . . the virginal aspect of this virgin is fused with her symbolic and real control over the rather non-virginal principles of fertility and reproduction."

On the other hand, but still related to the question of the importance of the festival of the Virgin of the Nativity for agriculture, throughout the agricultural cycle there are countless occasions when tensions and conflicts erupt among individuals and groups within the district. These involve such problems as disputes over land boundaries, conflicts over the use of water for irrigation, and seemingly countless episodes of the destruction of (usually small) sections of the cultivated field of one family by the herd animals of another. The various district-level officials in Pacariqtambo serve as the final, local arbiters in these disputes.

I would suggest that the gathering of people from throughout the district in the town of Pacariqtambo at the beginning of each agricultural season provides an important opportunity both for people to renew and reassess their relations with one another and for the officials and the *ayllus* of Pacariqtambo to reassert their dominance through two of their principal saints, San Pedro and the Virgin of the Nativity, over the surrounding villages. This is accomplished not only by the representation of the hierarchy of saints *within* Pacariqtambo, which emerges during processions and other events in the festival, but also by virtue of the fact that a saint from the outside (San Esteban) pays his respects especially to two saints of the town of Pacariqtambo at this time (this is the only occasion when the patron saint of a neighboring district or provincial capital visits a settlement within the District of Pacariqtambo). The presence of San Esteban in Pacariqtambo serves to validate and reinforce the dominance of the saints of the town of Pacariqtambo over those of the surrounding villages (see Poole, 1984:310–311; Sallnow, 1987:158–162).

One other aspect of the reciprocal visits between San Pedro and San Esteban is of special interest here. This concerns the *ayllu* sponsorship in Pacariqtambo of the visit by San Pedro to Yaurisque and the reception of the image of San Esteban in Pacariqtambo. (I should point out that I do not know who or what social group in Yaurisque is responsible for that community's share of these festivities.) The *cargo* for the festival of San Pedro in Pacariqtambo is shared by three *ayllus* of the upper moiety: Quinhuara, Aqchakar, and Qarhuacalla Primero. The *cargo* ideally rotates over a three-year period among these three *ayllus* (Urton, 1986).

It is of some significance for this study that Aqchakar and Qarhuacalla Primero are two of the *ayllus* responsible for the sponsorship of these reciprocal visits between San Pedro and San Esteban. These two *ayllus* are groups for which we have historical documentation identifying certain of their members as local elites in early colonial times. That is, Aqchakar (Anchacari in the Callapiña Document) was the *ayllu* with which Rodrigo Sutiq Callapiña was said to have been affiliated in 1569. It also appears, as mentioned earlier, that Manqo Qhapaq was thought to have been the ancestor of Aqchakar *ayllu* by virtue of the fact that Rodrigo successfully claimed him as his patrilineal ancestor. Qarhuacalla (Caruacalla) was the *ayllu* affiliation of Rodrigo Sutiq Callapiña's maternal great-grandfather, Kilaku Yupanki Inka. These local elites in Pacariqtambo all had connections—as descendants of the class of Inkas-by-Privilege—with members of the provincial seminobility in other communities in the area around Pacariqtambo (e.g., Yaurisque, Paruro, and Huanoquite) as well as with members of the Inka nobility in Cuzco.

With these data, we may now address the question of the possible significance of the annual visits between San Pedro and San Esteban as they may indicate traditional patterns of interactions between social and political groups in Pacariqtambo and Yaurisque in the past. I would hypothesize that these reciprocal visits, sponsored by three *ayllus* of the upper moiety in Pacariqtambo, represent the means whereby elites in Pacariqtambo and Yaurisque continued to interact with each other as they perhaps had done in pre-Hispanic times for a variety of ritual and political purposes. The means for continuing these (hypothetical) interactions was the translation of what would have been earlier visitations and interchanges (whose precise character we cannot specify) in the form of annual visits between the patron saints of these two communities. Sallnow (1987:88–99) has argued persuasively for the existence of similar examples of the reconstitution in colonial times of (presumed) pre-Hispanic pilgrimage networks. The Inka origin myth, as recounted by elites in Pacariqtambo and Cuzco in the mid- to late sixteenth century, may incorporate an account of these traditional practices in terms of the journey of the ancestors who, after their emergence from Pacariqtambo/Tampu T'oqo, traveled from Pachecti to Pallata and Haysquisrro (i.e., Yaurisque) on their way to Cuzco.

This hypothesis receives some support from a reconstruction of genealogical connections between the descendants of Inka nobility in Pacariqtambo and those in Yaurisque from the sixteenth to the middle of the eighteenth century. This documentation concerns, once again, the Callapiña family. Figure 4 summarizes references in the historical documents to members of the Callapiña family who served as governors and/or *caciques principales* in Pacariqtambo and Yaurisque from 1568 to 1760. The figure shows that Callapiñas served as authorities in Pacariqtambo from the 1560s to the end of the 1600s; they then disappear from positions of authority in

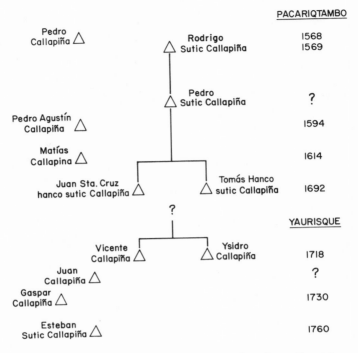

Fig. 4. *Caciques principales* of the Callapiña family in Pacariqtambo and Yaurisque (1568–1760)

Pacariqtambo and appear as governors and *caciques principales* in Yaurisque from the 1710s to the 1760s.

The data in figure 4 should not be taken to mean that the Callapiña family disappeared from Pacariqtambo altogether at the end of the 1600s, for individuals by this name are mentioned in censuses recorded in Pacariqtambo in 1836 (A.D.C., *Tesorería Fiscal del Cuzco*, no. 3), and there are even a few people who have this surname in Pacariqtambo today (however, there are many more Callapiñas who live in Yaurisque). It appears that the Callapiña family suffered a decline in its fortunes or status in Pacariqtambo at the end of the 1600s, as there are no references to political authorities by this name in the community after the beginning of the 1700s.

The ties between members of the Callapiña family in Pacariqtambo and Yaurisque may represent one set of genealogical, social, and political connections that has traditionally been reaffirmed and renewed in the visitations between San Pedro and San Esteban at the beginning of the period of planting, in August and September.

The Ritual Circuits of San Andrés and the Celebration of Cruz Velakuy

As an agricultural community whose livelihood depends primarily on the success of the crops, the rhythms of life in Pacariqtambo are built around the maturation cycles of plants and the succession of tasks required in planting, tending, and harvesting the crops. Following the period of planting, which begins in earnest during the month-long period of the reciprocal visits between San Pedro and San Esteban, there are two festivals that are celebrated within the district today that have particular significance in marking the period of the maturation of the crops: the festivals of San Andrés (November 30) and the day of the Finding of the Holy Cross (May 3); the latter is referred to as Cruz Velakuy in communities throughout the Andes. San Andrés marks the official end of the planting season, while Cruz Velakuy marks the official beginning of the period of the harvest (the harvest is usually completed by late June).

The celebrations of San Andrés and Cruz Velakuy are tied to each other over the (approximately) five-month period from late November to early May by (1) the natural agency of the beginning and end points of the period of the growth and maturation of plants at this particular location and altitude in the Andes; (2) the economic motivation of the production of crops both for household consumption and marketing; and (3) the ritual-symbolic expression that comes about by way of the movement of wooden crosses from inside the town of Pacariqtambo to the outside, at the end of planting, and from the outside back into town, at the beginning of the harvest. I have discussed the first two elsewhere (Urton, 1986, n.d.a). I will focus here on the third element: the annual movement of crosses between the town of Pacariqtambo and the outside.

As is common in other communities in the Andes, Pacariqtambo has a number of crosses that are placed on hilltops around the community during the period that the crops are maturing. The crosses are said to protect the crops from hail and other damage. In Pacariqtambo, the crosses are erected on hilltops around the district at the time of San Andrés, and they are removed from the hilltops—to be placed inside the church in Pacariqtambo—on Cruz Velakuy. The harvest begins soon after the crosses have been brought back into town, on May 3.

It is essential to point out that there are seven crosses that belong to different groups in the community today; five of the crosses are the responsibility (and corporate property) of *ayllus* of the upper moiety (one each for Nayhua, Qarhuacalla Primero, and Qarhuacalla

Segundo, and two for Quinhuara); two crosses belong to *ayllus* of the lower moiety (San Miguel and Pumatambo). The two fifth *ayllus*— Qarhuacalla Segundo and Pumatambo—have the major *cargos* for their respective moieties for the celebrations of the festivals of San Andrés and Cruz Velakuy (Urton, 1986).

There are two characteristics of the annual movement of the crosses that are important for our consideration: the first involves the role of moiety-level groupings of *ayllus* in transferring the crosses to hilltops around the district at the end of planting; the second concerns the role of the fifth *ayllus* of the moieties in the sponsorship of the festivals of San Andrés and Cruz Velakuy.

To explain fully the significance of the ritual circuits on the day of San Andrés, when the crosses are taken out of town and erected on the hilltops, I must first clarify two points concerning the ideology and symbolism of the moieties in Pacariqtambo. As mentioned earlier, it is said today that there were only two "*ayllus*" in Pacariqtambo at the beginning of time: Hanansayaq (of the upper part) and Hurinsayaq (of the lower part). Each of the moieties is considered to have originated at a certain place near town. These origin places are identified with two rock outcrops that are located just above and on the edge of town, to the northeast and southeast. The origin place of the upper moiety is identified as a rock outcrop to the northeast of town called Niñut'ankana (place for the child to lie down); the origin place of the lower moiety is a rock outcrop to the southeast of town called Intikis (your sun; plate 9).

The second point of clarification concerns the fact that each moiety has a patron under whose divine guidance and protection the *ayllus* of the moieties conduct their joint public affairs. The patron of the upper moiety is the Niñu Jesús (Child Jesus), whose day in the Christian calendar is December 25; the patron of the lower moiety is the Virgin of the Assumption, whose day of celebration is August 15. The care of the statues of these figures, which are kept in the church in Pacariqtambo, is the joint responsibility of all of the *ayllus* of their respective moieties. As we will see in a moment, when the *ayllus* of one or the other of the moieties carry out a public activity, they do so under the patronage of these divine sponsors.

With these two points of clarification concerning the moieties in mind, we can now turn to a discussion of the ritual circuits during the festival of San Andrés. On the morning of the day of San Andrés (November 30), the *ayllus* of the upper moiety that have the responsibility for crosses carry their crosses and the image of the Niñu Jesús from the church in Pacariqtambo up to the rock outcrop of Niñut'ankana (i.e., the origin place of Hanansayaq). From Niñu-

Plate 9. Pacariqtambo and the origin places of the upper and lower moieties: *a,* Pacariqtambo; *b,* Niñut'ankana (upper moiety); *c,* Intikis (lower moiety)

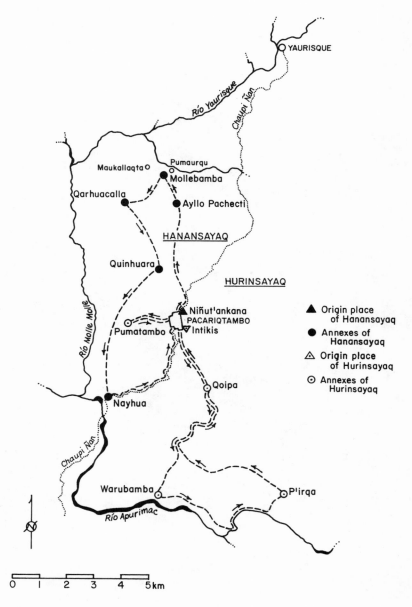

Map 5. The moiety origin places and the ritual circuits of San Andrés

t'ankana, the *ayllus* set off northward on a three- or four-day pilgrimage that will take them on a circuit of the territory of the upper moiety. During this ritual circuit, the *ayllus* erect their crosses on hilltops within the territory of the upper moiety and they visit the annexes along the way (see map 5). On the same day, the *ayllus* of the lower moiety carry their crosses and the image of the Virgin of the Assumption to the rock outcrop of Intikis, the origin place of Hurinsayaq. From here, the *ayllus* undertake a ritual circuit of the territory of the lower moiety, visiting annexes and erecting crosses on hilltops along the way.

The return of the crosses to the church in Pacariqtambo at the end of the agricultural season on the day of Cruz Velakuy (May 3) does not take place in formal circuits or ritual journeys, as at the time of San Andrés. Rather, the members of each *ayllu* that has a cross go to the place where it stands in the countryside and carry it back into town—bedecked with wild flowers—where it is fêted for several days and nights at the house of the *ayllu* member who has the *cargo* for the cross that year.

The local pilgrimages, or ritual circuits, that take place during the festival of San Andrés incorporate all of the social and residential groups within the district into a "community"—through their respective moiety groupings—by acting on a set of shared symbols through ritual at a certain time of the year. It is important to take note of the fact that people in Pacariqtambo *say* that San Andrés (November 30) is the official end of the planting season and the beginning of the period of hoeing and tending the maturing plants. Although planting can (and often does) continue somewhat beyond San Andrés, the point seems to be that this ritual serves as a means of signaling that a certain threshold in the agricultural cycle has arrived and seeks to orchestrate the activities of people in moving to the next stage and set of tasks in the agricultural cycle. I think that one reason that this kind of public "orchestration" is needed is because the planting of the crops must be accompanied by a change in overall herding patterns within the district. That is, the herd animals can no longer be allowed to pasture wherever they will; rather, they must be kept out of the fields that have recently been planted.

In summary, as is apparent from map 5, the ritual circuits of San Andrés essentially describe, or define, the territory of Pacariqtambo along two sets of boundaries: one—the boundary between the moieties within the territory—is along the route of Chaupi Ñan; the other is along the borders between Pacariqtambo and the outside.

We should elaborate further on the roles of the two fifth *ayllus* of

Pacariqtambo—Qarhuacalla Segundo and Pumatambo—in the rituals of San Andrés and Cruz Velakuy in relation to the fact that these two *ayllus* have the status of border groups in the overall organization of *ayllus* and annexes in the district. What is important to stress concerning the nature of the *cargos* in the case of the two fifth *ayllus* is that these *cargos* alternate during the course of the year between a *cargo* holder who lives *inside* Pacariqtambo and one who lives *outside*, in the village of the same name as the *ayllu*. This alternation coincides with that in which the crosses themselves are inside Pacariqtambo for part of the year and outside for the other part. That is, while the crosses of Qarhuacalla Segundo and Pumatambo are inside the church in Pacariqtambo (from May 3 to November 30), the *cargo* holders for the crosses are members of these *ayllus* who live in the town of Pacariqtambo; when the crosses are on the hilltops, outside of town (from November 30 to May 3), the *cargos* are in the hands of *ayllu* members who live out in the villages. This pattern of alternation occurs only in the cases of Qarhuacalla Segundo and Pumatambo.

What is important to note with respect to the alternation of the *cargos* of the fifth *ayllu* is that up until the beginning of the present century, Pachecti was the fifth *ayllu* of the upper moiety. Therefore, it is likely that up until relatively recent times, Pachecti would have had the principal *cargo* for the upper moiety for the celebrations of the festivals of San Andrés and Cruz Velakuy. I should point out that I do not have documentary evidence that confirms that *ayllu* Pachecti did, in fact, have this *cargo* in earlier times; however, the documents from Pacariqtambo (and elsewhere) seldom mention which *ayllu* had the *cargo* for which festival (as pointed out earlier, the Spanish clergymen who were responsible for overseeing these ritual activities in villages were generally not interested in such fine points of the local ritual calendars).

Regardless of whether Pachecti or Qarhuacalla Segundo—two *ayllus* whose associated villages are located near each other in the north of the district (see map 3)—had the *cargos* for these festivals in the past, the first segment of the ritual circuit undertaken by the *ayllus* of the upper moiety on the day of San Andrés would have proceeded with the crosses and the image of the Child Jesus from the rock outcrop of Niñut'ankana northward, along Chaupi Ñan, up to Pachecti, Mollebamba, and Qarhuacalla, all of which are located just above the Yaurisque River. This river has traditionally served as the boundary between the *ayllus* of Pacariqtambo and groups to the north.

What I find particularly interesting and compelling about the circuits of San Andrés for the problems that we are concerned with in this study is the (to me) striking coincidence between the following two images: on the one hand, that of a contemporary ritual in which the *ayllus* of the moiety of Hanansayaq in Pacariqtambo make a journey, along with a "miraculous child" (the Niñu Jesús), from the rock outcrop that was the origin place of the upper moiety northward to the area of Pachecti. On the other hand, that emerging from the mythohistorical tradition from the latter part of the sixteenth century in which the ancestors of the Inkas are said to have been born from a rock outcrop at Tampu T'oqo, within the territory of the upper moiety of Pacariqtambo, from where they set off on a journey to the north; at the first stopping place, Pachecti, a child was conceived from the union of one of the pairs of·ancestral siblings. The coincidences in the types of *personages* (ancestors or divine children, and "upper moiety people") as well as the *places* (rock outcrops and the village of Pachecti) present in these two traditions are, I think, suggestive of a strong continuity between an important mythohistorical tradition and contemporary ritual practice in the Pacariqtambo area.

My argument concerning the significance of the "continuity" that seems to link these two traditions is that the ritual is here reinforcing, explicating, and renewing the identification and cohesive relations among the people who live in the area of Pacariqtambo. I would argue that the ritual circuits of San Andrés represent the "appropriation" of Catholic ritualism for local purposes. This appropriation, or subversion, of the dominant tradition was probably motivated by two important considerations; the first, which was based primarily on an economic interest, was the need to effect some coordination of the agricultural and herding activities among settlements within the district; and the second was the desire on the part of the *ayllus* of Pacariqtambo to maintain their dominance over the annex villages within the district. Regardless of what motivated these practices, the result was the promotion of the identification of the native population of the district as a privileged group in regional "history;" that is, theirs was the territory from which the Inkas had originated at the beginning of time.

Royal Incest, Divine Conception, and the Birth of History at Pachecti and Waynakancha

The next major festival in the district occurs one week after San Andrés, on December 8; this festival centers on a pilgrimage to the local shrine of the Virgin of the Conception. The actual setting for this festival is the chapel in the Hacienda Waynakancha, which is located in the Yaurisque River Valley, just to the north of Pachecti, Mollebamba, and the ruins of Maukallaqta (see map 3). This pilgrimage is quite well attended, with celebrants coming from communities throughout the surrounding area, including Pacariqtambo, Yaurisque, and Huanoquite.[2]

It should be noted from the beginning of this discussion that the festival of the Virgin of the Conception celebrates the conception of the Virgin Mary, not that of the Christ Child. This point will be of importance when we return to a consideration of the symbolism of this festival in the local ritual calendar. Another point of clarification concerns the timing of the festival. That is, the celebration of the Virgin of the Conception (December 8) occurs soon after the completion of planting, just as the newly planted seeds begin to sprout.

The sponsorship of the festival at the shrine of the Virgin of the Conception in Waynakancha is undertaken by two parties. On the one hand, the owners of the Hacienda Waynakancha—the Pardo family—host the participants. They provide much of the food and drink consumed by the pilgrims, and, most important, the owners of the hacienda permit the pilgrims to view the image of the Virgin that adorns the wall of their chapel (see below). On the other hand, the principal duties involved in actually celebrating the festival, such as arranging for the transportation of the priest (who lives in Yaurisque) to Waynakancha, hiring bands and recruiting dancers, and contracting for the use of special ritual drinking vessels (*k'eros* and *k'usilluqs*), are undertaken by *cargo* holders who are residents of the nearby incorporated community of Mollebamba–Ayllo Pachecti.[3]

The object of veneration at this festival is a dark, somewhat amorphous image, said to represent the figure of the Virgin of the Conception, which appears on one of the stucco walls of the chapel in the Hacienda Waynakancha (plate 10). People today say that this image appeared miraculously on the wall of the chapel "about forty years ago." Although we cannot say for certain, I would suggest that this accounting of the antiquity of the image of the Virgin of the Conception probably represents a structural value (equivalent to "a long time ago," or "a lifetime ago") rather than indicating an absolute chronological period beginning at a precise date in the past.

There are certain data, in fact, that allow us to suggest a much greater antiquity not only for the Hacienda Waynakancha itself but also for the ritual observance of the festival of the Virgin of the Conception in the Yaurisque-Pacariqtambo area. The earli-

Plate 10. Pilgrims at the image of the Virgin of the Conception, Waynakancha. Photo by Jean-Jacques Decoster

est reference that I am aware of to the existence of the Hacienda Waynakancha dates to 1689; at that time, the hacienda was identified as the property of a doña María de Béjar and her two sons, Francisco and Diego Henrríquez (Villanueva, 1982:466). The earliest reference available to me of the celebration of the festival of the Virgin of the Conception in the area of Yaurisque-Pacariqtambo dates to 1772 (A.A.C., "Informaciones:" ff. 19v, 68). However, in 1790, one of the two chapels within the parish of Yaurisque was devoted to Our Lady of Guainacancha (Waynakancha). At that time, the chapel contained an image of the Virgin of the Purification (Oricaín, 1906 [1790]: 364).[4] Therefore the appearance of the im-

age of the Virgin on the wall of the hacienda chapel probably occurred after 1790. In an inventory of the religious paraphernalia in
the church in the town of Pacariqtambo, which dates to 1836–1865,
there are references to both a statue and an altar of the Virgin of the
Conception (A.A.C., "Fábrica de la iglesia de San Pedro de Paccarictambo:" ff. 1–4).

Although these references attest to the contemporaneous existence of the Hacienda Waynakancha, a cult of the Virgin of the
Purification at Waynakancha, and a cult of the Virgin of the Conception in Pacariqtambo by 1790, the references do not, in fact,
explicitly connect the Hacienda Waynakancha and the Virgin of the
Conception at such an early date. What is crucial for my argument here, however, is, on the one hand, the long history of the
celebration of the festival of the Virgin of the Conception in the
Pacariqtambo area, and, on the other hand, the sponsorship of this
festival by both the Hacienda Waynakancha and the community of
Mollebamba–Ayllo Pachecti for at least "forty years."

It is especially important in relation to the interpretation of
the events that occurred during the early stages of the Inka origin
myth to reflect on the fact that Ayllo Pachecti—along with its
near-neighbor Mollebamba—has the *cargo* today for the festival of
the Virgin of the Conception at the Hacienda Waynakancha. Recall that during the early part of the journey of the Inka ancestors from Tampu T'oqo to Cuzco, the first child of the Inkas was
conceived in the incestuous union between Manqo Qhapaq and
Mama Oqllu; this conception occurred at Waynakancha (i.e., Guanacancha; Sarmiento, 1942 [1572]: 52).[5] I would argue that the sponsorship, beginning "forty years ago," by Ayllo Pachecti of the festival
of the Virgin of the Conception at the Hacienda Waynakancha is
more than a fortuitous coincidence. It represents, I think, an important episode in the process of the syncretism of Catholic symbolism
and ritualism with local colonial-period, and perhaps pre-Hispanic,
mythohistorical traditions and geopolitical relations in the Pacariqtambo area, the earliest version of the latter of which is recounted
explicitly in the Inka origin myth.

We have, in this instance, an excellent example of the process of
syncretism and (I would argue) appropriation, which are similar to
that described in the following quotation from Sallnow's study of
pilgrimages in the circum-Cuzco region: "Miraculous [Christian]
shrines do not emerge onto religious tabulae rasae but into a historically configured ritual topography, a preexisting pattern of sacred
sites from which they must draw their significance. It is precisely in
their determinate relatedness, in time and space, with local ritual

centers, with earlier sacred locales, and with one another, that their contingent quality becomes significant," (Sallnow, 1987 : 89). These comments provide an appropriate introduction to a summary of the material discussed in this chapter.

Summary

The relevance of the material on rituals discussed here for the more general concerns of this study seem to me to be two overriding trajectories in the three ritual practices described. These two "trajectories"—by which I mean dominant themes in the combined meanings of, and motivations behind, the three rituals—are, first, an explicit relationship between ritual and agricultural cycles; and second, a larger and more inclusive association between the annual ritual and agricultural cycles and local strategies for reproducing mythohistorical traditions *through* syncretism.

The relationship between ritual and agricultural cycles can best be elaborated by constructing a table showing the relationship between the segments of these two annual cycles (i.e., ritual and agricultural) that I have emphasized here (table 7).

Table 7 illustrates what I think is a significant correlation between a set of pilgrimages and ritual circuits carried out annually in Pacariqtambo and a series of critical events in the annual sequence of tasks required in producing the crops that are the basis for the maintenance and reproduction of households throughout the district. The care of, and concern for, the crops is one of the principal considerations in the organization of activities in the district today, as it has been in the past. The sequence of agricultural tasks, which is closely tied to the herding cycle, is (as I have become aware from my own experiences living in Pacariqtambo) the most meaningful framework for the accommodation to life in any one of the villages in the district.

The coupling of a sequence of important moments in the agricultural cycle with a succession of elaborate, districtwide festival celebrations, especially when these involve pilgrimages and other forms of ritual travel requiring people to alter their mundane patterns of moving between house and field and travel instead to special places within (or immediately across the borders of) the district, charges these times with powerful symbolic meanings and *mythical metaphors*. It is to the question of the historical content of those mythical metaphors to which we now turn in elaborating the second "trajectory" of the rituals summarized in table 7.

What I find compelling in terms of a linkage among the rituals

Table 7. *Correspondences between the Ritual and the Agricultural Calendars*

Date	Focal Saint/Festival	Agricultural Task
August 8	San Pedro visits San Esteban in Yaurisque	Planting
September 8	San Esteban visits San Pedro for festival of the Virgin of the Nativity	Planting
November 30	Ritual circuits of San Andrés (erection of crosses on hilltops)	End of planting
December 8	Pilgrimage to the Virgin of the Conception at Hacienda Waynakancha	Seeds sprout; begin hoeing
May 3	Crosses returned from hilltops to church in Pacariqtambo	Begin harvest

included in table 7, which are by no means all of the festivals celebrated within the district (see Urton, 1986), is that each coalesces a different set of aspects of, on the one hand, agricultural practice and, on the other, symbolic and metaphoric components drawn from both Roman Catholicism and mythohistorical traditions relating to the origin of the Inkas. Perhaps the best example of this synthesis is the celebration of the festival of the Virgin of the Conception, which occurs near the places where the first Inka was conceived and born by "natural" means (i.e., rather than by the miraculous emergence from a cave), and at the time when the newly planted seeds are beginning to germinate in the soil. I would emphasize that we do not find here a separation, or hierarchy, of these meanings and intentions (e.g., as in the "masking" of an aboriginal correlation between agriculture and traditional mythology by a veneer of Roman Catholic symbols); rather, there is here a complete blending and syncretism of the various traditions involved.

What we find in the material discussed in this chapter, then, is evidence of a remarkably complex strategy and record of syncretism in which the annual agro-economic cycle is attuned *thematically* to the linear sequence coursing through, and uniting, two mythohistorical traditions, one "indigenous" (i.e., the Inka origin myth), the other "exogenous," or imposed (i.e., the rituals, symbols, and legends connected with the Christian deities and saints).[6]

From this point of view, we can now state tentatively a local theory of "historicity," that is, of how people think about history. In Pacariqtambo, history is the product of the synchronic and diachronic discourse, often, but not always, verbalized in "mythohistories," between the material conditions of life (e.g., the agropastoral cycle) and ritual practice.

I would conclude by observing that what we appear to have arrived at here is a notion similar to what Sahlins proposed concerning the resolution of the apparent impasse that has often been thought to exist between structure and history: "Culture may set conditions to the historical process, but it is dissolved and reformulated in material practice, so that history becomes the realization, in the form of society, of the actual resources that people put into play" (1981:7).

As I have argued here, one of the "actual resources" that has traditionally been put into play in the construction of history in Pacariqtambo is the mythohistorical identification of this community as the origin place of the Inkas. This resource has been called on by people in Pacariqtambo at least since the time of Rodrigo Sutiq Callapiña.

6. Conclusions

An Interpretation of the Inka Origin Myth from the Point of View of Pacariqtambo

In the first part of these conclusions, I will focus on the second of the two questions that were posed in chapter 1 as the objectives of this study: What light can we shed on the interpretation of the Inka origin myth on the basis of an understanding of the historical and ethnographic materials from the town and region of Pacariqtambo itself? I will address this question from two perspectives; the first concerns the journey of the ancestors from Tampu T'oqo to Cuzco; the second will focus on the status of the ancestors and of the ten nonroyal *ayllus* that were formed at Pacariqtambo.

The Concretization of Boundaries in the Journey of the Ancestors

In the origin myths recorded by Sarmiento de Gamboa, Cabello Valboa, and Murúa, the ancestors traveled from Pacariqtambo to Cuzco, stopping at several places along the way. After their emergence from Tampu T'oqo, these places included Pachecti, Waynakancha, Tamboquiro, Pallata, Haysquisrro, Quirirmanta, Wanakauri, Matawa, and Wanaypata. As stated earlier, I think that we can identify Tampu T'oqo with the archaeological site of Pumaurqu, and Haysquisrro with the town of Yaurisque.

I would argue that the journey of the ancestors can be divided into the following stages, each associated with a different set of boundaries in the mythic and geographical space between Pacariqtambo and Cuzco: (1) Tampu T'oqo → Yaurisque; (2) Yaurisque → Wanakauri; and (3) Wanakauri → Cuzco (see fig. 5). *Stage 1* represents the movement of the ancestors from within the territory of the upper moiety of Pacariqtambo to a point along the boundary between the moieties, that is, Pallata and the foot trail of Chawpi Ñan, and on to a place just outside the territory of Pacariqtambo (i.e., Yaurisque). *Stage 2* represents the movement from Yaurisque, which, in the quadripartite division of the valley of Cuzco, was located within the quarter of Kuntisuyu, to the mountain of Wanakauri; Wanakauri overlooks Cuzco and stood on the boundary between Kuntisuyu and Qollasuyu (the two quarters that together made up the lower moiety of Cuzco). *Stage 3* represents the movement from Wanakauri, within the lower moiety of Cuzco, to the place in the center of the city where the upper and lower moieties (as well as the forty-one *ceques*) converged (i.e., Wanaypata, the temple of Qorikancha).

The three stages of the journey of the ancestors were structured similarly with respect to three characteristics. First, each stage represents the movement from one part of a dual division in the geopolitical organizations of the territory around Cuzco to the border with its opposing, or complementary, part. In the sequence of these transitions as interpreted in figure 5, the first was from the upper moiety to the border with the lower moiety of Pacariqtambo; next, from the quadrant of Kuntisuyu to its border with Qollasuyu within the lower moiety of Cuzco; and finally, from the border of the lower moiety of Cuzco to its point of articulation with the upper moiety. Second, each stage in this sequence brought the ancestors one step closer to Cuzco, from a point on the periphery to a hill overlooking the Cuzco Valley, and finally, to the center of the city itself. And third, at the end point of each stage of the journey, one of the ancestral brothers was separated from the entourage. At Yaurisque, Ayar Kachi was sent back to Tampu T'oqo, where he was entombed; at Wanakauri, Ayar Uchu was transformed into stone; and at Wanaypata, Ayar Awka was transformed into a pillar. Seen in the light of the first two features, which are shared by the three stages of the journey, it is clear that the death or transformation of the three Ayares brothers represents the concretization, and consecration, of the boundaries of successive configurations of bilateral and concentric geopolitical divisions within the territory between Pacariqtambo and Cuzco.[1]

On one level, then—that of the journey of the ancestors—the origin myth is concerned explicitly with the problem of identifying and defining boundaries within, and on the borders of, the valley of Cuzco. At this level, I would interpret the origin myth as a mythohistorical, and perhaps an "ethnological," construction in which the central structural features and problematical relationships in the organization of the imperial city of Cuzco were identified (e.g., the relations between Cuzco and the outside, the age-based system of ranking the *ayllus* among the four quarters, and the *ayllu* and

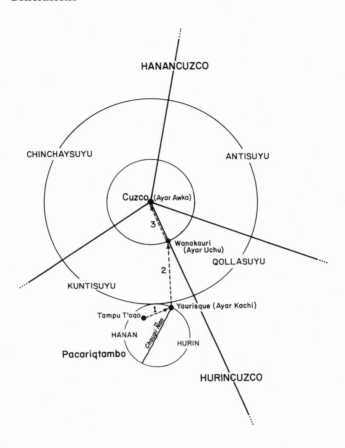

Fig. 5. Geopolitical boundaries and the journey of the ancestors

moiety organizations in Cuzco); these institutional structures and
relational categories were then rephrased, as a historical problem-
atic, from the point of view of an "appropriate" outside group (i.e.,
one that shared essential features of its sociopolitical organization
with Cuzco). This rephrasing—or projection—represented a means
of universalizing these issues and of situating the rationale for these
especially complex and potentially problematical forms of organization in Cuzco in terms of regional space and remote times. Viewed
at a distance, and decontextualized of the specific geographical,
historical, and individual composition of these institutions and

forms of organization within the Cuzco Valley, they were represented, and thus confirmed, as autochthonous elements in social
history, parts of the landscape. In short, the organization of Cuzco is
represented, and thereby rationalized, in the origin myth, as though
it were what we call *"history"*—as both a product and a synthesis of
primordial geopolitical, social, and ethnic divisions and interrela-
tionships within the region.

The Role of "Border People" in the Inka Origin Myth

Building on these interpretations, I would suggest that the ancestors
and the ten nonroyal *ayllus* that were created at Pacariqtambo represented additional expressions of and perspectives on the preoccupa-
tion with boundary groups and other such social, temporal, and
spatial "border" categories in the organization of Cuzco and of the
empire as a whole. The expressions of this concern in terms of
the central actors and social groups in the myth of origin include the
following: (1) the Inkas-by-Privilege, who were linked to the Inka
nobility by marriage alliances and who formed ties between the
nobility in Cuzco and the commoners throughout the empire (in
Pacariqtambo, this group included such characters as Kilaku Yupanki
Inka and Qoya Qori Kuka); (2) the ten nonroyal *ayllus* of Cuzco,
which occupied an intermediary status between the royal *ayllus*
(*panaqas*) in Cuzco and the *ayllus* of local ethnic groups—such as
the Maskas of Pacariqtambo—outside of Cuzco; and (3) Manqo
Qhapaq and Sinchi Ruq'a, the first two Inka kings, who, from the
point of view of Sarmiento's noble informants in the 1570s, lived in
a remote time, were born outside of Cuzco, and, therefore, were
problematical characters because they were at the same time for-
eigners and ancestors.

Each of the individuals or groups identified above represents a
boundary or linking category in the historical and geopolitical organization of the empire. I would argue that Sarmiento's informants
perceived these individuals and groups as, on the one hand, central
figures in the mythohistorical formations and transformations of
the empire (in which case we should add the name of Pachakuti Inka
to the list) and, on the other, as points of potential stress, tension,
contradictions, and conflict in the organizational structures and
ideological principles underlying the empire. From this perspective,
we can see that the concern with these boundary individuals and
groups was perhaps the motivation for the particular structural features incorporated in the journey of the ancestors as represented in

figure 5. The journey was a theoretical construction and a normative expression of the relationship between geopolitical boundaries and border categories in the overall organization of the empire.

Colonial Transformations of the Origin Myth

These interpretations of the origin myth, which have as their basis an understanding of the political and territorial relations among the *ayllus* of Pacariqtambo today and between elites in Pacariqtambo and Cuzco in the sixteenth century, permit us a final reflection on the questions of why and how the place of origin became concretized to the area of Pacariqtambo and what role the local elites played in these processes.

I would first reemphasize that, on the basis of the ethnohistorical evidence, we cannot say for certain whether or not the accounts of the origin of the Inkas from Pacariqtambo represent a pre-Hispanic tradition or whether these accounts appeared only in the early colonial period, perhaps as both a response to, and a "maneuver" within, the increasingly historicized and concretized representations of Inka mythohistory that were being formulated during the mid- to late sixteenth century. A better understanding of the comparative archaeological records in Cuzco and Pacariqtambo, and especially a thorough study of the sites of Pumaurqu and Maukallaqta (such as that promised in the preliminary studies by Bauer, 1987, n.d.), should provide insights into this problem. But archaeological records and interpretations notwithstanding, what we have found in the data discussed here is the record of an extremely creative and complex process of the use and manipulation of the personalities and categories of the origin myth by members of the provincial elite in Pacariqtambo, as well as by descendants of both the royal and nonroyal *ayllus* of Cuzco.

I have suggested that one of the principal themes in the origin myth was the crucial, and potentially problematical, status of certain boundary categories of individuals and groups, such as the Inkas-by-Privilege, who often served as *caciques principales* (*kurakas*) in the organization of the Inka empire. The collapse and destruction of the empire did not, in fact, result in the immediate disappearance of such boundary or intermediary categories and positions. For example, the *caciques principales* continued to play an important role as intermediaries between local *ayllus* and the Spanish in the colonial system of governance (see Saignes, 1987; Spalding, 1984; Stern, 1982*a*, 1982*b*).

Local *caciques principales*, like Rodrigo Sutiq Callapiña, and the lineages that they represented in early colonial times, were both skilled and practiced in the arts of occupying and representing such intermediary, boundary positions in the local and regional political systems within their respective territories. Their knowledge and skills served them well until the rules of governance, and the expectations placed on them, changed radically with the reforms instituted by Viceroy Toledo in the mid-1570s. These new expectations (e.g., new forms of tribute and higher demands on local labor for state projects) placed even greater stress on the *caciques* and worked to erode their standing with both the Spanish and the local *ayllus* (Espinoza Soriano, 1960:62–65; Ramírez, 1987:602–607, 610; Rowe, 1957:156). It was just as these processes began to reshape life in Andean communities (during the late 1560s–1570s) that members of the urban and rural elite began to try to reposition themselves to confront these new realities. It was under these circumstances, for instance, that Rodrigo Sutiq Callapiña sought to establish firmly his—and his descendants'— privileged status within the newly historicized and concretized political geography of the circum-Cuzco region.

It is in the context of the slow yet inexorable transformation of the urban and provincial political landscapes in the early colonial period that the Inka elites began to recount to the Spaniards the "history" of the Inka empire. The central change that occurred in the manipulations of Inka mythohistorical traditions in the early colonial period was in terms of the motivations for which such manipulations were carried out. That is, the central motivation was no longer one of situating both the elite lineages and their allied, subordinate *ayllus* within the integrated, hierarchical framework of kinship and ethnic relations and administrative structures whose point of reference was the Inka in Cuzco; rather, the central motivation became the attempt by local elites to obtain privileged status and exemptions for themselves and their families.

While the motivations for rehearsing Inka mythohistory changed radically from the 1530s to the 1570s, both the personnel and the geopolitical categories to which these traditions referred remained essentially intact until the end of this period. Therefore, I would conclude that the Inka origin myth centering on Pacariqtambo probably *does* represent an old, well-attested mythohistorical tradition of origin—or at least that it was one *interpretation* of the origin of the Inkas, which was formulated and maintained by populations near Cuzco, within the quarter of Kuntisuyu, in pre-Hispanic times. As this interpretation was recounted in the context of the new geopolitical, ideological, and cosmological realities of the early colonial world, and as it became concretized and historicized in the official histories recorded by the Spanish chroniclers, it became increasingly irrelevant for ethnic groups and *ayllus* outside of the immediate area of the territory that became identified as "Pacariqtambo"; as a consequence, its relationship to other formerly complementary, or competing, interpretations (such as that of the tradition of origin centering on Lake Titicaca) became ever more tenuous.

Final Reflections

There are a number of questions of a more general, theoretical nature that are raised by this study. Two of the principal questions are, first, what transformations took place in native ideology and culture as a result of the domination of Andean populations by an aggressively expansive, literate Western society? and second, what, after all, can we—or ought we to be able to—say about the nature of, and the relationship between myth and history?

As to the first question, there were a number of contradictions and transformations that emerged in native Andean ideology and society as a consequence of the colonial experience. Prominent among these were changes in the basis of sociopolitical and economic organization from an intimate connection between kinship and descent as *primary* relations and idioms for the exercise of authority and their replacement by the Spanish-dominated colonial administrative bureaucracy. What I have primarily been concerned with here is the investigation of the manipulation of mythohistorical traditions for political ends as a reflection of these changes in the nature and sources of power in one Andean community. I have argued here that there was a close connection between the processes of the appropriation of mythohistorical traditions as "history" and native reformulations of sociopolitical hierarchies in response to colonial domination. These attempts—by such individuals as Rodrigo Sutiq Callapiña—at strategic accommodations to, and appropriations of, the new forms of legitimation and sources of power indicate that Andean peoples were not passive, inert objects in these new historical and political processes; rather, they were active participants in the production of their own histories through their engagement of the Spaniards at all levels of sociopolitical integration (i.e., from that of the descendants of Inka nobility in Cuzco to the various local terrains controlled by the ethnic lords).

Finally, we return to the central questions of this study. What is myth? What is history? And where within this determination do we locate what I have referred to here as "mythohistory"? These questions all turn on the more fundamental issue of who, in the end, constructs truth in history? Concerning the nature of myth and history in the Andes, I would maintain the position stated at the beginning of this study with regard to references in the colonial documents to people and events before the time of Spanish contact; that is, since we have no written records from before the conquest, *we* have no grounds on which to evaluate the truth of any assertion made by a native to a Spaniard with respect to such persons or events. Thus, these utterances can only be viewed in an indeterminant way with respect to whether or not they represent what Western historiography recognizes as history as opposed to myth; that is, they must be classified ambiguously as "mythohistorical" commentaries.

This position does not mean, however, that we are unable to approach the more fundamental question of who constructs truth in history. As far as I am aware, truth in history has always and everywhere been determined by those who hold power. However, rather than reducing the study of history to an attempt to determine whether or not what is *recognized* as historical truth is, in fact, *true*, it seems that the more important tasks of an anthropologically informed study of history are, first, to seek to understand the processes whereby historical representations are formulated; second, to try to determine the relationship between these formulations and the social, political, economic, and religious contexts within which they are produced and sustained; and third, to examine the careers of these historical formulations and representations as they are reproduced and reformulated—over both the short and the long terms—by the individuals and collectivities (e.g., *ayllus*, ethnic groups, and classes) for whom they constitute conditions of, and for, action.

In the case at hand, this process of historical incorporation and transformation began in the early colonial period with such individuals as Rodrigo Sutiq Callapiña and Domingo Pascac, who recited into the Spanish documents both the myth of a certain history and the history of a myth. The origin myth was called up again during the eighteenth century in the Callapiña Document, which was compiled in 1718 by Vicente and Ysidro Callapiña. Parts of the myth continued to be reproduced in the transformed idioms of Roman Catholicism by the nineteenth- and twentieth-century owners of the Hacienda Waynakancha, by the residents of the small village of Pachecti, who sponsored the festival of the Virgin of the Conception, and by the towns of Pacariqtambo and Yaurisque, who continued to carry their patron saints to visit each other every year.

What is particularly interesting is that even in its newly historicized form, the Inka origin myth did not cease to be manipulated for
wider (i.e., state) political and personal ends, nor did it become inac-
cessible to the people in Pacariqtambo as a source of identification
and a point of mythohistorical orientation. For example, in 1964, the
president of Peru, Fernando Belaúnde Terry, visited Pacariqtambo in
a gesture that was blatantly intended to incorporate into the foundations of his newly installed government the legitimacy afforded by
contact with the origin place of the Inka empire. Like Pachakuti
Inka "returning" to the cave of Tampu T'oqo at the beginning of his
own reign, Belaúnde Terry flew into the plaza of Pacariqtambo in a
helicopter. After receiving a wooden *vara* (a staff of office used in the
cargo system), Belaúnde helicoptered back to Cuzco.

But the mythohistory of this community is sustained today not
only from the outside. As recalled by one of my principal informants
in Pacariqtambo, the story (translated from the Quechua) goes as
follows:

> Now we are going to talk. In Pacariqtambo there appeared near
> this town all together the three Inka brothers, the "Hermanos
> Ayares"; this place is called Tampu T'oqo. From the ancient
> time of the appearance of the Hermanos Ayares from Pacariq-
> tambo, the Inkas lived in the ruins built there in Maukallaqta
> and Pumaurqu. There, there are beautiful ruins, made by the
> Inkas, of stone that was brought to that place from Murunpam-
> pawayqo [valley of the spotted plain]; from that quarry they car-
> ried stones to Maukallaqta and they made beautiful buildings. In
> that time, how lovely was the hill of Pumaurqu near Molle-
> bamba; how beautiful was that great hill. There, the Inkas slept
> in the late afternoon in the entrance [guarded by] . . . the beau-
> tiful little pumas; the beautiful, labyrinthine little thing lying at
> the bottom of the valley. In that opening was the entrance to the
> Inka's house. There, we have finished speaking.

Appendix
The Callapiña Document

[1]

*Presst*on

En la Gran Ciud del Cuzco en dos diaz del mes de Mayo de mill y quinientos y sesenta y nueve años Ante El muy Magnifico Señor Licenciado Juan Ayllon Theniente de Correxidor y Juzticia Mayor en ella y su Jurisdiccion por su Magestad y en presencia de mí Sancho Ortis de Orus Exno Publico y del Cavildo de ella Parecio Dn Rodrigo Sutec Callapiña y presenta la Peticion y Preguntas Siguientes.

*Petic.*on

Muy Magnifico Señor Dn Rodrigo Sutec Callapiña Casique Principal y Governador del Ayllo An Reducido en el Pueo de San Pedro de Pacaritambo de la Prova de Chilques y Masquez = Hijo Lexitimo

[1v]

de Dn Franco hanco Sutic Callapiña Casique Principal y Governaor que fue del dho Pueo de Pacaritambo contenido en la Real Cedula de Armas que pressento Con el Juramto y Solemnidad en dro Nessesario = Y de Da Angelina Cori Coillor Paresco Ante Umd. Y Digo que el dho mi Padre fue Ynga Prinzipal y decendiente por Linia Recta de Baron de *Manco Capac* [all emphases are mine] Primer Rey y señor Natural que fue deestos Reynos del Peru y Como F[?]nl Gano la Real Cedula de Armas que presento = Y La dha mi madre fue hija Lexitima de Dn Martín Yupanqui hijo de quilaco Yupanqui Ynga del *Ayllo Caruacalla* de dho Pueo de Pacaritambo y de la Coya Coricoca que murieron Gentiles = Y el dho Dn Franco hanco Sutic mi Padre fue hijo Lexitimo de Don Fernano Auquisutic y de Da Mencia Paucar ocllo y a difuntos de la Cassa y Sangre Real del dho Manco Capac y como tales desde sus Padres y Progenitores Por ser Como fueron yngas Prinzipales y conosidos por tales desde El tpo del ynga nunca xamas sirvieron en Tambos ni en otros Servicios ni pagaron Tributos antes si fueron acotados y Respetados de todos los Yngas Prinsipales del dho Pueo y de los de las ocho Parroquias deesta Ciud de lo qual me combiene hacer una Provansa para perpetua memoria Como major Aya Lugar de dro. y que se Examinen los testigos que presentare por las preguntas Siguientes =

(1) Primeramente Si conosen al dho Don Rodrigo Callapiña Casique Principal del *Ayllo Anchaca* del Pue° de Pacaritambo y Conosieron a D^n Fernando Auquisutec Abuelo del dho D^n Rodrigo Sutec Callapiña y a D^n Fran^{co} hanco sutec su Padre del dho D^n Rodrigo = A D^n Martín Yupanqui Ynga del *Ayllo Caruacalla* Abuelo Materno del dho D^n Rodrigo y si tubieron noticia del Ynga *Manco Capac* Senōr Natural que fue de estos Reynos y de quilaco Yupanqui Ynga y de la

[2]

Coya Coricoca que murieron Gentiles.

(2) Y si Saven que el dho D^n Fran^{co} hanco sutec fue Casado y Velado segun orden de la Sta Madre Yglecia Con Dª Angelina Coricoyllor y de este Matrimonio hubieron y Procrearon por su hijo Lexitimo al dho D^n Rodrigo Sutec Callapiña a quien le Criaron y alimentaron llamando les de hijo y el a ellos de Padre y Madre y en esta Posecion asido y es avido y tenido y Comunm^{te} Reputado Sin auer cosa en contrario.

(3) Y si Saven que la dha Dª Angelina CoriCoyllor Madre del dho D^n Rodrigo Sutec Callapiña fue hija lexitima de Don Martín Yupanqui hijo de quilaco Yupanqui Ynga del *Ayllo Caruacalla* Reducido en el Pue° de San Pedro de Pacaritambo y de la Coya Cori Coca que murieron Gentiles = Y Durante el Matrimonio que contrajeron entre el dho D^n Martín Yupanqui y Dª Franca Sayri huvieron y procrearon por tal su hija lexitima a la dha Dª Angelina Coricoillor = Y la críaron y alimentaron llamandola de tal hija y en esta opinion y fama asido y es avida y tenida y comunm^{te} Reputada.

(4) Y si sauen que el dho D^n Franco hanco Sutec Padre del dho D^n Rodrigo Sutec Callapiña fue hijo Lexitimo de D^n Fernando Auquisutec y de Dª Mencia Paucar ocllo ya difuntos y por ser los suso dhos Parientes muy Sercanos y decendientes por Linia Recta de Baron de *Manco Capac* Primer Rey y Señor Natural que fue de estos Reynos del Peru Le onrro la Cesarea Magestad del Señor Emperador Carlos quinto con la Cedula de Armas que ba por Cauesa de esta filiación Para el y Para todos sus decendientes y los que fueron de la Sangre y Prosapía del dho *Manco Capac.*

(5) Y si sauen que por ser tales Yngas Principales y de Sangre Real y Prosapía del dho Ynga *Manco Capac* los dhos D^n franc^{co} hanco Sutic y de Dª Angelina Coricoyllor fueron Respetados y acatados de los Yngas de las ocho Parroquías de esta Ciudad del Cuzco y el dho D^n Franc^{co} hanco Sutic fue y es Casique Principal y Gouerna^{or} del dho Pue° de

[2v]

San Pedro de Pacaritambo y la dha Dᵃ Angelina CoriCoyllor como hija Lexitima de Dⁿ Martín Yupanqui y nieta de quilaco Yupanqui Ynga del *Ayllo Caruacalla* asi mesmo fue Respetada de los Principales y los unos y los otros desde el Tpo del Ynga fueron Conosidos por Tales Yngas nobles y como Tales Nunca pagaron Tributo ni jamas sirvieron en Tambos ny en otros Servicios Personales Antes fueron Governadores de su Pueº.

(6) Y si sauen que todo lo suso dho Es Verdad Publico y notorio Publica Vos y fama y despues de lo suso dho En la Ciuᵈ del Cuzco en dose diaz del mes de Mayo de mill y quinientos y sesenta y nueve años

Testigo

En Precensia y con Asistencia del Muy Magnifico Señor Lizenciado Juan Ayllon Theniente de Correxᵒʳ y Justicia Mayor en ella Por su Magᵈ y de mi el pressente Exⁿᵒ Publico el dho Dⁿ Rodrigo Sutic Callapiña Para la dha Ymformacion Presento por testigo a Don *Diego Atao Yupanqui* y a *Santiago Aucamira* yngas Naturales de esta Ciuᵈ de los quales y de Cada uno de ellos Se tomó y Reciuió Juramento en forma Segun dro. Por Lengua de hernanº de Morales Ynterprete General por Dios y por Una Señal de Cruz En que Pusieron sus manos derechas y Prometieron de decir Verdad y al dho Juramento dijeron síjuro y Amen = Y lo que los dhos testigos y Cada uno de ellos Dijeron y de Pusieron es como se sigue.

(1) A la Primera Pregunta dixo q conosen y conosieron a los en ella Contenidos de las Preguntas Generales de la Ley que le fueron hechas y declaradas Dixeron que no le tocan ninguna de ellas y que el dho Dⁿ Diego Atao Yupanqui es de Edad de ochenta y sinco años y el dho Santiago Aucamira de Nouenta y tres años.

(2) A [la] Segunda pregunta = Dixo que como Vieron a Dⁿ Franco hanco Sutic y Vio que el suso dho fue Casado y Velado Segun orden de la Santa Madre Ygᵃ con Dᵃ Angelina Cori Coyllor y de este Matrimonio hubieron y procrearon por su hijo Lexitimo a Dⁿ Rodrigo Callapiña a quien Criaron y alimentaron Llamandole de hijo y el a los suso dhos de Padre y Madre Y en esta Poseción y fama asido y es avido y tenido y Comunmᵗᵉ Reputado Sin aver cosa en contrario

[3]

Y esto Responden.

(3) A la tercera Pregunta dijeron que Conosieron trataron y Comunicaron a Dᵃ Angelina Coricoyllor Madre del dho Dⁿ Rodrigo Sutic Callapiña y Saue por auerlo Visto que la Suso dha fue hija Lexitima de Don Martín Yupanqui hijo de quilaco Yupanqui Ynga Casique Prinzipal del *Aillo Caruacalla* del dho Pueº de Pacaritambo y de la

Coya Cori Cuca que murieron Gentiles y que Durante el Matrimonio que contrajieron entre el dho Dⁿ Martín Yupanqui y D^a franca Sayri huvieron y procrearon por tal su hija Lexitima a la dha Dª Angelina Coricoyllor y a vista de estos testigos la Criaron y alimentaron llamandola de Tal hija y en esta Poseción fama y opinión asido y es auida y tenida y Comunm^{te} Reputada sin auer cosa en Contrario y esto Responden.

(4) A la quarta Pregunta dijeron que Conosieron trataron y Comunicaron familiarmente a Don Fernan^o Auqui Sutic Casique Principal y Govern^{or} que fue del Pue^o de San Pedro de Pacarictambo y a Dª Mencia Paucar ocllo ya Difuntos y sauen por auerlo Visto que los suso dhos fueron Casados y Velados segun orden de la Sta Madre Yg^a de Roma y que les Vio hacer Vida Maridable En uno y de este Matrimonio huvieron y Procrearon por su hijo Lexitimo al dho Dⁿ Fran^{co} hanco Sutic contenido en la Cedula Real de Armas que ba por Cauesa de estos Autos y lo Críaron y Alimentaron llamandole de hijo y el a ellos de Padre y Madre y en esta Poseción opinión y fama asido y es auido y tenido y Comunm^{te} Reputado Sin auer Cosa en Contrario y esto es lo que Saue de esta pregunta y Responde a ella.

(5) A la quinta pregunta Dijeron que en Conformidad de todo lo que a dha[?] declarado en las preguntas Antecedentes Sauen por auerlo Visto que el dho Dⁿ Rodrigo Sutic Callapiña y dho su Padre Y Abuelo decendientes por Linia Recta de Baron del Ynga *Manco Capac* Primer Rey y senor Natural que fue de estos Reynos y Como tales an sido y fueron Respetados y acatados de los Yngas Nobles de esta Ciu^d y

[3v]

les an admitido en Actos Publicos onrrandose con ellos y que sauen Assimismo que desde sus Antepasados An sido Gouernadores del dho Pue^o de San Pedro de Pacarictambo = Y an oido decir por tradición Antigua a sus mayores y mas Ancianos Como el dho Ynga *Manco Capac* Nació de Una Ventana que llaman *Tambo Toco* que esta en una Peña tres Leguas de esta Ciu^d en el Valle de Tambo y junto a esta Peña esta otra peña y en ella otra bentana que llaman *Marastoco* = Sauen asimesmo que el dho Dⁿ Rodrigo Sutic Callapiña y sus Padres y Abuelos desde el Tpo del Ynga fueron y son todos Avidos y tenidos por tales Yngas Nobles y decendientes del dho *Manco Capac* Ynga = Y Como tales nunca Pagaron Tributos Ni siruieron en Tambos ni hisieron mitas ni Seruicios Personales antes fueron Gouernadores de su Pue^o y esto Responden.

(6) A la sesta Pregunta dijeron = que todo lo que an dho y declarado es la Verdad Publico y Notorio Publica Voz y fama SoCargo de los Juramentos que an hecho en que se afirmaron y Ratificaron y

no firmaron porque dijeron no sauer firmolo El dho Theniente de Correx[or] con el dho Ynterprete Lizenciado Juan Ayllon = hernando de Morales = Sancho de Orue Ex[no].

Testigo

En la Ciu[d] del Cuzco a dose diaz del mes de Mayo de Mill y quinientos y sesenta y nueve años, Ante el Muy Magnifico Señor Licenciado Juan Ayllon Theniente de Correx[or] y Justicia Mayor en ella Por su Mag[d] y de mi El presente Excriuano = El dho D[n] Rodrigo Sutic Callapiña Para la dha su Ynformacion Presento por testigo a D[n] *Domingo Pascac* Yndio Natural de esta Ciu[d] del Cuzco Recidente en la Parroquía de Señor San Blas y D[n] *Franc[co] Rauraua* de la Parroquía de Señor San Geronymo de las Quales por Lengua E ynterpretación del dho Ynterprete se les Reciuio Juramento y lo hisieron Cada uno de Por si con los dedos de sus manos derechas por Dios nro. Señor y por una Señal de la Cruz en forma de dro. y so Cargo del qual prometieron de decir Verdad y Siendo preguntados por el tenor de las Preguntas del dho Pedimiento dijeron lo Siguiente.

(1) A la Primera Pregunta Dixeron que Conosen y Conosieron a los En ella Contenidos y trataron y Comunicaron a Cada uno en su Tpo y esto Responden = de las Preguntas Generales de la Ley que le fueron

[4]

hechas y declaradas = Dixeron que no les tocan ninguna de ellas y que el dho D[n] Domingo Pascac es de Edad de Nouenta y ocho Años y D[n] Franc[co] Rauraua de Ciento y seis años y esto Responden =

(2) A la Segunda Pregunta = Dixeron que Sauen por auer lo visto que Don Franc[co] hanco Sutic Padre del dho D[n] Rodrigo Sutic Callapiña fue Casado y Velado Segun orden de la Santa Madre Yglecia con D[a] Angelina Coricoyllor y de este Matrimonio huvieron y Procrearon Por su hijo Lexitimo Al dho D[n] Rodrigo Sutic Callapiña a quien le críaron y alimentaron llamandole de hijo y el a ellos de Padre y Madre y en esta Poseción an sido y es avido y tenido y Comunmente Reputado sin auer cossa en Contrario y esto Responden.

(3) A la Tercera Pregunta = Dixeron que sauen por auer lo visto quando mosos Como quilaco Yupanqui Ynga del *Aillo Caruacalla* del Pue[o] de Pacaritambo y que este fue Casado Segun su Ley con la Coya Cori Cuca y que murieron Ambos Gentiles en Tpo de *Guayna Capac* Ynga y que ubieron y Procrearon Por su hijo a D[n] Martín Yupanqui quien se Baptiso despues que entraron los Españoles En este Reyno y a este D[n] Martín Yupanqui Conosio trataron y Comunicaron Estos testigos y que se Caso y Velo Segun Orden de la Santa Madre Yg[a] con D[a] franc[ca] Sayri a quien Conosieron asimesmo y les Vieron hacer Vida Maridable y de este Matrimonio huvieron por su

hija Lexitima a la dha Dª Angelina Cori coyllor y la Criaron y alimentaron por tal Confesando la por su hija y esto Responden.

(4) A la quarta pregunta = Dijeron que Conosieron a Dⁿ fernanᵒ Auqui Sutic y a Dª María Paucar ocllo marido y muger Lexitimos y sauen por auerlo Visto que los suso dhos fueron Casados Lexitimamte y de este Matrimonio ubieron por su hijo Lexitimo Al dho Dⁿ Francᵒ hanco Sutic y que por tradición Antigua sauen el suso dho y su Padre y Abuelos son y fueron de la Sangre Real y prosapía del Ynga *Manco Capac* Primer Rey y señor Natural que fue de esta Tierra y por esta Razon La Catholica y Sesarea Magᵈ del Señor Emperador Carlos quinto Le honrro Con la Cedula Real de Armas que ba por Caueza de esta filiación Para El

[4v]

y para todos sus decendientes y los que fueron de la Sangre y prosapía del dho Ynga *Manco Capac* y esto responden—

(5) A la quinta pregunta = Dixeron que saven por ver lo visto que por ser tales Yngas Principales de la Sangre Rˡ del dho *Manco Capac* Ynga Los Dhos Dⁿ Francᵒ hanco Sutic y Dª Angelina Coricoyllor fueron respetados de los Yngas Nobles de las ocho Párroquías de esta Ciuᵈ del Cuzco = Y que el dho Dⁿ franᵒ hanco sutic fue casique principal y Governaᵒʳ del dho Pueᵒ de S. Peᵒ de Pacaritambo = Y la dha Angelina Cori coyllor como hija lexitima de Dⁿ Martín Yupanqui Y nieta de quilaco Yupanqui de *Ayllo Caruacalla* asimesmo fue respetada de los Principales Yngas y los unos y los otros save que desde el tpo del Ynga fueron Conosidos por tales Yngas nobles y como tales nunca pagaron tributos ni jamas Sirvieron En Tambos ni en otros servicios Personales y que tan solamente fueron Governadores de su Pueᵒ y aillos y esto responden—

(6) A la sesta Pregunta = Dixeron que todo lo que an dho y declarado Es Publico y Notorio Publica vos y fama y la Verdad so cargo del Juramᵗᵒ que fho tienen en que se afirmaron y Ratificaron y no firmaᵒⁿ porque Dijeron no Saver firmaronlo El dho theniente de Corregᵒʳ y Justicia Mayor y dho Ynterprete = Licenciado Juan Ayllon = hernando de Morales = Sancho de Oruz Exⁿᵒ

Testigo

En la Ciuᵈ del Cuzco a dose dias del mes de Mayo de mil y quinientos y sesenta y nueve años Ante el muy Magnifico Señor Lzᵈᵒ Juan Aillon theniente de Correxᵒʳ y Justicia Maᵒʳ en ella por su Magᵈ y de mi el presente Exⁿᵒ el dho Dⁿ Rodrigo Sutic Callapiña para la dha Ymformᵒⁿ presento por testigos a Dⁿ *Juan Pisarro Yupanqui* Yndio Natural de esta Ciuᵈ del Cuzco a Dⁿ *Gonzalo llamac auca* Ynga Naturales de la Parroquía de Nra señora de Belén de los quales se les Recivieron Juramᵗᵒ por Lengua E ynterpretación del dho hernando de

Morales ynterprete y lo hisieron por Dios Nro. Señor y por una señal de Cruz Segun forma de dro. So cargo del qual prometieron de decir Verdad y siendo preguntados Por el tenor de las Preguntas del dho pedimento Dijeron lo siguiente—

(1) A la primera pregunta = Dijeron que conosen a todos los Conte

[5]

nidos en esta pregunta y especialmente al dho Dⁿ Rodrigo Callapiña que les presenta y esto responden—

(2) A la segunda pregunta = Dijeron que saven por aver lo visto Como Dⁿ franᶜᵒ hanco sutic fue casado y velado Segun Orden de la Santa Madre Ygª Con Dª Angelina Coricoyllor y les vio haser Vida Maridable en uno y de este Matrimonio huvieron y Procrearon por su hijo lexitimo al dho Dⁿ Rodrigo Callapiña a quien lo criaron y alimentaron llamando le de hijo y el a los dhos sus Padres de Padre y Madre y en esta opinion y fama asido y es avido y tenido y comunmᵗᵉ reputado sin aver cosa en contrario y esto Responden—

(3) A la tercera pregunta = Dixeron que conosieron trataron y Comunicaron a Dⁿ Martín Yupanqui Abuelo Materno del dho Dⁿ Rodrigo Sutec Callapiña y saven por aver lo oido desir a sus Padres y mayores que el dho Dⁿ Martín Yupanqui fue hijo de quilaco Yupanqui Ynga del *Ayllo Carualla* [sic] del

Pueᵒ de Pacaritambo y de la Coya Coricoca y que ambos murieron Gentiles y que vieron que el dho Dⁿ Martín Yupanqui fue casado y velado segun orden de la ssᵗᵗ Maᵉʳ Yglecia con Dª Francª Sayri y de este Matrimonio huvieron y procrearon por su hija lexitima a la dha Dª Angelina Cori coillor Madre del dho Dⁿ Rodrigo Callapiña y la criaron y alimentaron llamandola de hija y ella a los dhos sus Padres de Padre y Madre y en esta posecion asido y es avida y tenida y Comunmᵗᵉ Reputada y esto Responden—

(4) A la quarta Pregunta = Dixeron que consieron [sic] a Dⁿ Fernando Auquisutec y a Dª Mencia Paucar Ocllo y Saven fueron casados y velados Segun orden de la SSᵗᵃ Madre Ygª y de este Matrimonio Ubieron por su hijo Lexitimo al dho Dⁿ franco hanco Sutic, y que saven asimismo que

por ser el dho Dⁿ franᶜᵒ hanco Sutic, y dho Dⁿ Rodrigo Sutec Callapiña su hijo Parientes muy cercanos y desendientes de *Manco Capac* Señor Natural que fue de estos Reinos del Peru an acatado y Respetado a lo suso dhos

[5v]

Los mas Principales Yngas de esta Ciudad y que al dho Dⁿ Franᶜᵒ hanco Sutic Le honrro La Magestad Cesarea del Señor Emperador Carlos quinto Con una Cedula Real de Armas de su decendencia qu es la que esta al principio de esta filiación y esto Responden.

(5) A la quinta Pregunta = Dixeron que Sauen por auer lo Visto que por Cedula de su Magestad por ser Yngas Principales y de la Sangre Real y prosapía del Ynga *Manco Capac* los dhos Dn franco hanco Sutic = Dⁿ Fernanº Auquisutic Su Padre y demas sus Progenitores fueron Respetados y acatados En esta Ciuᵈ de los Yngas nobles y mas Principales de ella = Y que en los actos Publicos = Concurrían juntos y que por esta Razon y ser tan notoria su noblesa nunca pagaron tributos ni a Cubieron haser Seruicios En tambos ni otros ministerios y que Siempre fueron Governadores en su Pueº y esto Responden.

(6) A la Sexta Pregunta = Dixeron que todo lo que an dho y declarado y Publico y notorio Publica Vos y fama y la Verdad so Cargo del Juramᵗᵒ que fho tiene en que se afirmaron y Ratificaron y dijieron que no les tocan Las Generales de la Ley y que el dho Dⁿ Juan Pissarro Yupanqui es de hedad de mas de Ciento y Veinte años Y El dho Dⁿ Gonzalo llamac Auca Ynga de Nouenta y quatro Años y no Supieron firmar Y lo firmaron El dho theniente de Correxᵒʳ y Justicia maᵒʳ = y dho Ynterprete = Lizenciado Juan Ayllon = hernando de Morales = Sancho de Orue Exⁿᵒ =

Testigo

En la Ciuᵈ del Cuzco = a Dose dias del mes de Mayo de mill y quinientos y sesenta y nueve años Ante el muy magnᶜᵒ Señor Lizenciado Juan Ayllon Theniente de Correxᵒʳ y Justicia Mayor En el por su Magestad y de mi El presente Exⁿᵒ El dho Dⁿ Rodrigo Sutic Callapiña para la dha Ynformaon presento por testigos = a Dⁿ *Martín Natipi Yupanqui* y a Dⁿ *francº Apuranti* Ynga naturales de esta dha

[6]

Ciuᵈ que Reciden en el Pueº de Larapac de la Encomienda de Pedro Alonso Carrasco = de los quales se Reciuio juramento y lo hisieron por Dios Nro. Señor y por una Señal de Cruz Segun forma de dro. y Abiendo lo fho Cada uno de por si prometieron decir Verdad y siendo preguntados por lengua E ynterpretacion de hernanº de Morales ynterprete = Dixeron y declararon lo Siguiente.

(1) A la Primera pregunta = Dijieron que Conosen a Dⁿ Rodrigo Sutic Callapiña Casique Principal y Governᵒʳ del *Ayllo Anchacari* Reducido en el Pueº de Pacaritambo de la Provª de Chilquez y Masquez y Conosieron asimismo a Dⁿ Fernanº Auqui Sutic Abuelo del dho Dⁿ Rodrigo Sutic Callapiña y a Dⁿ Francº hanco Sutic Contenido en la Real Cedula de Armas que ba por Cauesa de esta filiacion = y Conosieron asimismo a Dⁿ Martín Yupanqui Abuelo materno del dho Dⁿ Rodrigo Sutic Callapiña y tienen Noticia por tradicion

Antigua del Ynga *manco Capac* Señor Natural que fue de esta Tierra y que nacio de una bentana que esta en una Peña en el Pue° de Pacaritambo tres Leguas de esta Ciu^d que llaman *Tamputoco* y Junto a este esta otra Ventana llamada *Maras toco* y que en Tpo de *Guascar ynga* Conosieron a quilaco Yupanqui Ynga del *Ayllo Caruacalla* de dho Pue° y a la Coya Cori cuca Vis Aguelos del dho D^n Rodrigo Sutic Callapiña que murieron Gentiles antes que los Españoles Pasasen a este Reyno Y esto Responden. Testig° De las Preguntas Generales de la Ley que les fueron declaradas = Dijieron que no les bocan ninguna de ellas y que el dho D^n Martín Natipi Yupanqui y Don fran^co Apuranti Ynga Son Compadres del dho D^n Rodrigo Sutic Callapiña y no por eso dejaran de decir la Verdad en lo que se les preguntare = Y que el dho D^n Martín Natipi Yupanqui es de hedad de Ciento y treinta y dos años y el dho D^n fran^co Apu

[6v]

ranti de Ciento y ocho años y esto Responden.

(2) A la Segunda Pregunta Dijeron que Sauen por auerlo Visto que D^n Fran^co hanco Sutic Padre del dho D^n Rodrigo sutic Callapiña fue Casado y Velado Segun orden de la SS^ta Ma^e Ygl^a Con Dª Angelina Cori Coyllor y de este Matrimonio ubieron y procrearon por su hijo Lexitimo al dho D^n Rodrigo Sutec Callapiña a quien le criaron y alimentaron llamandole de hijo y el a ellos de Padre y Madre y en esta Possecion asido y es auido y tenido y Comunm^te Reputado Sin auer auido Cosa en contrario Y esto Responden.

(3) A la Tercera Pregunta = Dixerion que assimesma Sauen Por auerlo Visto En Tpo del Ynga *Guascar* que quilaco Yupanqui Ynga del *Ayllo Caruacalla* del Pue° de S. Pe° de Pacaritambo contenido en esta Pregunta y Vis Abuelo Materno del dho D^n Rodrigo Sutic Callapiña fue Casado En su Gentilidad con la Coya Coricoca y que murieron Ambos Sin Baptisarse antes que los Españoles entraron en esta Tierra = Y que en aquel Tpo asilos Pa^s de estos testigos como los Yngas de los Pue^os del Contorno de esta Ciu^d Antes de la Reducción General le Respetauan y onrrauan al dho quilaco Yupanqui por ser de la Sangre Real y Generacion del Ynga = Y que asimismo el dho D^n Martín Yupanqui su hijo y Abuelo Materno del dho D^n Rodrigo Sutic Callapiña fue Conosido de los Yngas por noble y de la Sangre Real de los Yngas y que a Vista de estos testigos Lo sentauan los Yngas Principales despues de la Reduccion General de los yndios Juntam^te con ellos en Actos Publicos y que el dho D^n Martin Yupanqui se caso en dho Pue° de Pacaritambo con D^a fran^ca Sayri y se hallaron en su Casam^to Por auer ydo a dho Pue° Con sus Padres y despues los vio haser Vida maridable Lexitimamt^e de este Matrimonio Procrearon

por su hija Lexitima a la dha D^a Anjalina CoriCoyllor y la criaron y alimentaron por tal Comfesandola por su hija y esto Responden.

[7]

(4) A la quarta Preguna = Dixeron que Conosieron a Don Fernan^o Auquisutic Y a D^a Maria Paucar ocllo marido y muger lexitimos y Sauen por auerlo Visto que los suso dhos fueron Casados y Velados Segun orden de la Santa Madre Yg^a y de este Matrimonio hubieron por su hijo Lexitimo al dho D^n Fran^co hanco Sutic Su hijo y sus Asendientes fueron Conosidam^te de la Prosapia y Sangre del Ynga *Manco Capac* Primer Rey que fue de esta Tierra por Linia Recta de Baron y que por esta Razon la Magestad del S^a Emperador Carlos quinto le honrro con la Cedula Real de Armas que ba por Cauesa de esta filiacion y esto Responden.

(5) A la quinta Pregunta = Dijeron que Sauen asimesmo Por auer lo Visto que los dhos D^n Fernando Auquisutic Don fran^co hanco Sutic y dho D^n Rodrigo Sutec Callapiña por su Notoria Calidad y Noblesa y ser Como dho es de la Sangre y prosapía del Ynga *Manco Capac* Cada Uno en su Tpo fueron Respetados y obedecidos de los Yndios y estimados de los Yngas de los Pueblos Combesinos de esta Ciu^d, y que el dho D^n Fernan^o D^n Fran^co hanco Sutic y dho D^n Rodrigo Sutic Callapiña fueron Casiquez Principales y Governadores en dho Pue^o de Pacaritambo Susediendose unos en pos de otros y que por ser asi Conosidos desde El Tpo del Ynga nunca pagaron tributos ni Sirvieron en Tambos ni hisieron mitas ou otros Seruicios Personales como lo hasen los demas Yndios baladies y hatun Lunas y esto Respondieron.

(6) A la Sexta Pregunta = Dixeron que todo lo que an dho y declarado Es Publico y notorio Publica Vos y fama y la Verdad So Cargo del Juram^to fho en que se afirmaron y Ratificaron y no firmaron por no Sauen firmalo el

[7v]

dho theniente de Correx^or y justicia mayor y dho Ynterprete Lizenciado Juan Ayllon = hernando de Morales, = Sancho de Orue Ex^no.

Pressta^on

Despues de lo Suso dho En la Ciu^d del Cuzco a dose dias del mes de Mayo de Mil y quinientos y sesenta y nueve años Ante El dho El[?] Lizenciado Juan Ayllon Theniente de Correx^or En esta dha Ciu^d y su termino Parecio El dho D^n Rodrigo Sutic Callapiña y presento El Escrito Siguiente.

Pettip^on

D^n Rodrigo Sutic Callapiña Casique Principal y Governor del *Ayllo Anchacari* Reducido en el Pue^o de San Pedro de Pacaritambo Prov^a

de Chilquez y Masquez = Digo que yo tengo dala Ynformacion de lo
que articule en mi primer pedimento de la Qual tengo nessecidad
deella en Publica forma y manera que haga fee Para acudir con ella a
do[?] combenga ami dro. y para ello Umd Ynterponga Su autoridad y
decreto Judicial tal qual de dro Ser requiere Sobre que pido Justicia y
para ello Ua = Don Rodrigo Sutic Callapiña Auto =
Y Pressentado El dho S^{or} theniente mando que sele de como le pide y
que en ello ynterpone su autoridad y decreto Judicial tanto quanto
puede y con dro. deue = Y com vista de la ymform^{on} dada declaro al
dho D^n Rodrigo Sutic Callapiña por tal hijo Lexitimo de D^n Fran^{co}
hanco Sutic contenido en la Real Cedula de Armas que esta al principio de ella y de Dª Anjalina Cori Coyllor = y nieto Lexitimo de D^n
Fernan^o Auquisutic y de Dª Mencia Paucar ocllo sus Abuelos Paternos
y nieto de D^n Martín yupanqui y de Dª Fran^{ca} Sayri sus Abuelos
maternos y por uía de baron decendiento por linia Recta del ynga
Manco Capac Señor Natural q fu de estos Reynos y por Vía de Madre
de quilaco Yupanqui Ynga del *Ayllo Caruacalla* del Pue^o de Pacaritambo de la Sangre de los Yngas y Como tal deuer gosar de los
fueros Priuilegios franquesas Exempciones y Liuertades que gosaron
los dhos Sus Padres y ante pasados y gosan los Nobles decendientes
de los Yngas Señoras que fueron

[8]
De esta tierra Comforme a las Cedulas Reales despachadas Sobre
esta Razon y asi lo proueyo y firmo = Lisenciado Juan Ayllon =
Sancho de Orue Ex^{no} Publico y Cavildo. Concuerda Con su Original
que para esta eferto Ante mi Excriuieron D^n Juan Santa Cruz hanco
Sutic Callapiña = D^n Thomas hanco Sutic Callapiña = hermanos
E hijos Lexitimos que dijeron Ser de Don Pedro Sutic Callapiña
y Nietos de D^n Rodrigo Callapiña = y D^n Diego Chuyacama y
Don Geronymo Luna = y Don Geronymo = Lucas Cusiguaman y
Boluieron alleuar a su poder a que me Refiero y para que de ello con-
ste de pedimento de los suso dhos Doi el presente En el Pue^o de
Urcos de la Prov^a de quispicanche a Veinte y dos dias del mes de
Junio de mill y Seiscientos y nouenta y dos años Siendo testigos Pe^o
Alfonso del Castillo = El Alferes D^n fran^{co} Nauarrete y Mateo
Masias de la Peña presentes = Entre Renglones = que no Vale = tes-
tado = Ynga = no Vale = mas testado = del = fe = no vale = entre
renglones = c[r]on = y enmendado = fue respetada = Vale Y en
fee de ello lo signo y firmo = En testimonio de Verdad = fran^{co}[?]
Cauesudo Ex^{no} Publico Concuerda esta traslado con otro[?] traslado
q ant mi Exiuieron D^n Vizente Callapiña [y] Ysidro Callapiña bisnie-
tos que dijeron ser de Don Rodrigo Callapiña aquien lo bolui a en-

tregar uno y otro y para que consta con el presente de su pedimento. En Balle de Urubamba Marquesado de Oro pas[a] en dies y ocho dias del mes de Nobiembre de mil setecientos dies y ocho años ciendo testigos Ysidro de Quiñas Joseph Carrasco presentes =

Paso Anttemi Y El Fiz, De ello lo signo y firmo

En testimonio De su Verdad

Joseph xisnero
Exri[o] de Su Mag[d]

Notes

1. The Mythic Dimensions of Inka History

1. Any study of historical and ethnological materials in the Andes must inevitably confront the problem of the tremendous variation in orthography of the Quechua language that is found in the various documents. The orthography that I have employed here is a compromise—aimed at attaining a reasonable level of readability and intelligibility—between two systems, or standards. I have left certain well-known, Hispanicized words (e.g., Cuzco, Yaurisque, Pacariqtambo) in their commonly known orthography. The majority of Quechua words, personal names, and place names are rendered in the orthography of Cuzco-Collao Quechua, which is readily available in Antonio Cusihuamán's *Diccionario Quechua Cuzco-Collao* (1976). I have left proper names and toponyms in their original form in quotations so as not to litter these pages with what would be innumerable brackets.

2. I will not enter here into the debate on the nature of the deity Wiraqocha, or T'iqsi Wiraqocha, as represented in the Spanish chronicles. Suffice it to say that this was a central character (or set of characters) in imperial religious ideology whose exact attributes and nature in Inkaic thought are now difficult to retrieve. The reasons for this are primarily because the various chroniclers developed different understandings of this character, and because from the beginning of the colonial period there appears to have been a conflation of Wiraqocha with both the God of Western Christianity and the Christian concept of the Holy Trinity (Duviols, 1977; MacCormack, 1984; Pease, 1973; Rostworowski, 1983; Urbano, 1981, 1986, 1988).

3. The "pristine" states referred to here are the five ancient states (Mesopotamia, Egypt, China, the Mayan, and the Inkan) that are considered to have emerged through indigenous evolutionary development rather than, as with "secondary" states, from contact with a preexisting state-level society. There are numerous examples of secondary states that did not develop their own system of writing, but that adopted the script and writing system of a state with which they came into contact (see Goody, 1977; de Heusch, 1982).

4. There is no entirely satisfactory term for this narrative form. Allen uses

the phrase "mythic history" (1984), while Randall employs both "mytho-history" and "mythstory" (1987, n.d.). I have chosen to use "mythohistory" because this term seems to me to denote most clearly the potentially equal and simultaneous, and thus fully ambiguous, mythical and historical status of the accounts contained in these narratives.

5. For another study that takes a similar point of view on the grounding of mythohistorical analysis in local interpretations and ideologies, see Allen's excellent study of "mythic history" in the community of Sonqo (1984).

2. The Pacariqtambo Origin Myth in the Spanish Chronicles

1. Urbano's *Wiracocha y Ayar* (1981) contains a very useful compendium of the principal accounts of both the Lake Titicaca and the Pacariqtambo cycles of origin myths. Specific references to a number of these accounts are given at appropriate places in this text (see Acosta, 1987; Betanzos, 1968; Cabello Valboa, 1951; Callapiña, 1974; Cieza de Leon, 1967; Cobo, 1964; Guaman Poma de Ayala, 1980; Molina, 1943; Murúa, 1946; Pachacuti Yamqui, 1950; Polo de Ondegardo, 1916; Sarmiento de Gamboa, 1942; Toledo, 1920).

2. The measure used here is one league equals 5.5 kilometers. This appears to have been the standard length of the *legua común*, which was used for itinerary measures in sixteenth-century Spain (Chardon, 1980). This value accords reasonably well with what Hyslop found in a study of various Peruvian accounts of the league. Hyslop concludes that, although there is considerable variation in the documents, "leagues shorter than 4.1 km. or longer than 6.3 km. were probably rare" (1984:296).

3. While most of the Spanish chroniclers state that eight ancestors emerged from Tambo T'oqo at the time of creation, Cieza de León says that there were only six, three brothers and three sisters (1967 [1553]: 14–15). In some of the versions of the origin myth that I collected in Pacariqtambo, there were said to have been only three brothers, "Los Hermanos Ayares." The names most commonly mentioned for the three brothers in Pacariqtambo today are Ayar Manqo, Ayar Kachi, and Ayar Awka.

4. The sociopolitical and ritual organization of the imperial city of Cuzco was based on the division of the population of the valley of Cuzco into ten royal *ayllus* (called *panaqas*) and ten nonroyal *ayllus*. The royal *ayllus* were ideally composed of the descendants of the Inka kings, with the exception of the successor to the throne, who formed his own royal *ayllu* (Rostworowski, 1983; Zuidema, 1964, 1986). The nonroyal *ayllus* had their origins in the ten *ayllus* that were created by the ancestors at Pacariqtambo. The members of the royal and nonroyal *ayllus* of Cuzco formed a two-tiered hierarchy of noble lineages in the empire when opposed to the lineages of commoner *ayllus* outside of Cuzco (cf. Rowe, 1985a: 35–36).

5. Toledo says that the founder of Ayllu Sauasiray was a fierce man who came from Sutiq T'oqo (i.e., the lateral window at Tampu T'oqo from which

originated the Tambos Indians and Sutiq T'oqo Ayllu). Ayllu Antasayac was descended from a man named Quisco Sinchi. Ayllu Arayuchu (Ayarucho) was descended from the fourth ancestor, Ayar Uchu. The members of the latter *ayllu* were also known as Alqawisas, the name of the pre-Inkaic inhabitants of the valley of Cuzco (Toledo, 1920[1572]:132–143).

6. Cristóbal de Molina (el Cuzqueño) is one possible exception to this observation. Molina lived in Cuzco for some twenty-three years, from about 1556 to 1579. He was fluent in Quechua and perhaps served as translator for Archbishop Loaysa, who, in 1559, collected information on the Inkas from Inka *principales*, priests, and *khipukamayuqs*. Molina wrote an account of Inka beliefs and ritual practices entitled *Fábulas y ritos de los Incas* (1943 [1575]). He also apparently wrote a history of the Inkas, which has been lost. Porras Barrenechea suggests that Molina's *Historia de los Incas* may have been the source from which Sarmiento took much of the information in his own *Historia de los Incas*. However, Sarmiento's history was submitted to Toledo in 1572, whereas Molina apparently did not begin work on his own history until 1573 (Porras Barrenechea, 1986:350–351).

7. Cristóbal de Molina (1943[1575]:30–32) identifies Quesco (Quisco) *ayllu* as the fifth *ayllu* of Hurincuzco; this may refer to the same group as Ayllu Antasayac, which was founded by Quisco Sinchi (note 5). Molina identifies Uru (Oro) as an *ayllu* of Hanancuzco (see Rowe's discussion concerning the differences—or "discrepancies"—in the names of the fifth *ayllus* as given in the various accounts [1985a:38–41]).

8. In documents from the mid-sixteenth to the mid-seventeenth centuries, the territory of the Maskas was placed to the west of, and adjacent to, that of the Chillkis. The Chillkis, whose territory included Araypalpa, Paruro, Pocoray, and Aqcha, were said to have been moved into that area from Pacariqtambo by Tupa Inka (Poole, 1984:91–92). The modern-day province of Paruro was known until the nineteenth century as the Province of Chillques and Mascas (or Másquez). The colonial *repartimiento*—a nonterritorial grant of patronage over a group of Indians—of Pacariqtambo included some of the *ayllus* of the Maskas ethnic group (Poole, 1984:84, fig. 4).

9. As far as I am aware, the first person to try to identify the toponyms of the origin myth within the geographical territory of the modern-day district of Pacariqtambo was Luis A. Pardo (1946, 1957). Pardo, an archaeologist and the owner of the Hacienda Waynakancha, also gave the earliest complete descriptions of the ruins at Maukallaqta and Pumaurqu. Unfortunately, Pardo's map of the journey of the ancestors from Pacariqtambo to Cuzco contains many inaccuracies in the location of places along the route of the journey from Pacariqtambo (i.e., Maukallaqta) to Cuzco. Pardo concluded, as I have here, that Tampu T'oqo should be identified with the site of Pumaurqu and that Haysquisrro probably refers to Yaurisque (Pardo, 1957, vol. 1:32–47).

3. The Role of the Urban and Provincial Elite in Historicizing Inka Mythohistory

1. A transcription of this document follows:

Con fha, de 5 Sept⁻ al Sup⁻ Fcal de V.S., que en la Doct⁻ᵃ de Yaurisque de ese Partido existía un considerable numero de Yndios que alegaban ser Nobles, y que careciendo de docum⁻ᵗᵒˢ comprobantes de su noble linage habían ofrecido de palabra dar una información que justificase la verdad de su alegato.

Han sido muy repetidas, y estrechas las ordenes que se han dada para que lo verifiquen, y h⁻ᵗᵃ la pres⁻ᵗᵉ fha no lo han executado; lo que sin duda nos hace creer, que su posesión es ilegitima, y que, excepto a uno, otro, que ha protado, con juridica información, posesión de Nobleza, debemos colocarlos en la clase de Tributarios.

El hallanse ya vencido el tiempo en que debe procederse al entero de los R⁻ˢ Tributos nos impele a decir a V.S. que aguardamos mi pronto determinación, asi en la referida consulta, como en lo pral a que este oficio se dirige. Man. de Fonnegras, Bern⁻ᵈᵒ Ramos. (A.D.C., *Intendencia, Real Hacienda*)

2. My thanks to Eulogio Coronel González, who allowed me to copy some two hundred pages of original documents from the Coronel collection in 1985.

3. There is a curious historical inconsistency in the Callapiña Document with respect to the name of the town of Pacariqtambo. That is, there are several references in the material from 1569 to the "reduction" (*reducción*) of "San Pedro de Pacaritambo." For example, the community is referred to by this name on the first page of the document (Appendix A, p. 129). The problems here are, first, that the reduction that later became known as Pacariqtambo was not founded until 1571 (two years *after* the Callapiña Document was drawn up), and second, when the town *was* founded, it was originally called San Pedro de Quiñoca (Ulloa, 1909). Pacariqtambo was the name of a *repartimiento* of Indians (see note 8, chap. 2), some members of which were reduced into the town in question. In the historical documents available to me, the town is not commonly referred to by the name of Pacariqtambo until the mid-1590s. As the town of Pacariqtambo did not exist when the original legal proceeding recorded in the Callapiña Document took place (1569), the references in the material from 1569 to the reduction of *ayllus* into a town of this name probably represent emendations to the text that were made when the document was copied in either 1692 or 1718. The purpose of the emendations would probably have been to clarify the relationship between the *ayllus* mentioned in the original 1569 document and the town of Pacariqtambo, which had existed—and had been known by that name—for more than a century when the first copy of the 1569 document was made.

4. The eight witnesses, who testified in four pairs, are identified in the Callapiña Document as follows:

(a) Diego Atao Yupanqui (85 years old) and Santiago Aucamira (93 years old);

(b) Domingo Pascac (98 years old), parish of San Blas, and Francisco Rauraua (106 years old), parish of San Geronimo;

(c) Juan Pissarro Yupanqui (120 years old), parish of Belén, and Gonzalo Llamac Auca Ynga (94 years old), parish of Belén;

(d) Martín Natipi Yupanqui (132 years old), and Francisco Apuranti (108 years old). These last two men, who claimed to be *compadres* of Rodrigo Sutiq Callapiña, lived in the town of Larapac in the *encomienda* of Pedro Alonso Carrasco.

5. Randall's comments on Rodrigo Sutiq Callapiña's genealogy were made on the basis of his reading of a draft of the present work and comparing the genealogical history recorded in the Callapiña Document with that recorded in Cabello Valboa's account of the mythohistorical encounter between Kilaku Yupanki and Qori Qoyllur (Randall, *n.d.*).

6. Sarmiento gives the name of Ancovilca—also written Ancoallo—as the founder/ancestor of the lower moiety of the Chankas (Sarmiento, 1942[1572]:83–84). The name Ancoallo (or Hancoallo) may refer to a large ethnic confederation to the west of Cuzco known as the Ancku Wallokc (Navarro del Aguila, 1983 [1939]). This confederation included the Pokras, Wankas, and Chankas. There was also a large ethnic group called the Ancoyocondes who, at the time of the Spanish conquest, lived to the south of Cuzco and Pacariqtambo, in the area of what is today the Province of Chumbivilcas (Poole, 1987:260–261).

7. In the 1964 edition of Cobo's chronicle, the name of this *waka* is written "Tanancuricota" (1964[1653]:184). In his transcription of the material provided by Cobo on the *ceque* system of Cuzco, Rowe states that this name should read "Chañan Curi Coca" (Rowe, 1980:56).

8. Having lived in communities around Cuzco for several years, I can attest to the fact that age is a highly relative and variable trait of identity among older Quechua-speaking people. I have seldom gotten a precise and convincing statement of age from anyone who claims to be over fifty or sixty.

4. Ethnographic and Ethnohistorical Dimensions for a Local Interpretation of the Inka Origin Myth

1. Pacariqtambo maintained a complex festival-*cargo* system until the time of the Agrarian Reform. Until then, each of the *ayllus* and annexes had three *cargo* officials. On January 1, the *carguyuqs* (*cargo* holders) of the *ayllus* and annexes would meet in the morning in the churchyard in Pacariqtambo, where their offices and the hierarchical relations among the offices were reconfirmed by the district governor (Urton, 1984). In the afternoon, the *carguyuqs* made the two- to three-hour trip to the provincial capi-

tal of Paruro for reconfirmation by the subprefect of the province. The latter process integrated the *cargo* officials of Pacariqtambo into the regional hierarchy of *cargo* holders throughout the Province of Paruro.

2. Ayllo Pachecti had only one member in 1831 (A.D.C., *Tesorería Fiscal del Cuzco*, Libro no. 2). In the combined census of *ayllus* Ccarhuacalla, Pachecti, and Rumiticti in 1850, there was a total of only three *ayllu* members (A.D.C., *Tesorería Fiscal del Cuzco Libros de Matrículos*, Prov. de Paruro, no. 4). The lands of Ayllo Pachecti were taken over by the Flores family, which owned the Hacienda Rumiticti (A.D.C., *Libros del Concejo Provincial del Cuzco*; A.M.A.C.; Paccarectambo, exp. #4281, 1964).

3. The document in question is transcribed below [my emphasis]:

Fecha: 17.V.1568
Don Francisco Paucar, principal del Pueblo de *Pachicti* y Sebastian Curillo, principal del pueblo de *Caruacalla* y Bautista Princoncho del pueblo de *Quinuara* y don Luis Sutic, principal del pueblo de *Acchacara*[?] y don Diego Calla Paucar, principal del pueblo de *Cuño* y don Diego Chalco, principal del pueblo de *Cuypa*, que todos se incluyen en el repartimiento de Pacaritambo de la encomienda de don Luis Palomino, sujetos a don Pedro Calla Piña su cacique y senor principal. Dan poder a Garcia de Esquivel en la Real Audiencia de Charcas y a don Luis Paucar, Francisco Rauraua, Bernabe Chalco, Andrés Yaure y don Alonso Chalco, que estan ausentes, a todos juntos para que representandolos pidan a Su Magestad y a su Real Audiencia de Charcas que nombren al dicho Pedro Calla Piña por su cacique principal y señor de todo el repartimiento de Pacaritambo, como lo es y le pertenece de derecho por linea recta y "espela y espiue" a don Alonso Cauncho cacique que al presente es por Maña y los desagravien de los agravios que les hace el dicho Cauncho.
Presentan contra Cauncho memoriales firmados de los principales.
Fecho en Cusco (A.G.N.; personal communication, Luis Miguel Glave)

4. The document in question concerns the assigning of lands in the territory of Pacariqtambo to Pasqual Quispicapi, a native of Paruro, by Francisco de Valverde Montalbo, judge and magistrate of the Province of Chilques and Masques (i.e., Paruro). This document is at present in the collection of the Coronel family. Part of the text from which this extract and translation were made is given below:

y luego este dho día mes y año [26 November 1643] fuy al asiento de ynquelbamba y manchaybamba metí en poseción al dho don pasqual quispicapi una fanegada de tierras en los dhos assientos que lindan con las tierras de pedro gamarra y mas tres fanegadas en el asiento de chinchaypucyo y poaponco = mas ocho topos en el asiento de albiray linda con las tierras de don Joan rauraua y por otra parte con chuchipiray y por la parte de arriva con un cerro llamado *biracochay* y por la parte de abaxo con las tierras de uaylla y hayosapata metí en poseción al dho don pasqual quispicapi de tres fanegadas linda por la parte de arriva con las tierras de los *yndios de quinaorai* y por la parte de abaxo con las tierras de don martín callapiña y por un lado con las tierras de los *yndios de acchacaray y anchacalla.* (My emphasis)

5. A transcription of the text from which this translation was made follows: "En los asientos de Mollebamba y otros nombres se midieron las tierras de dicha hacienda lindando por una parte con tierras de Pedro Gamarra que las divide una quebrada llamada Guaman uras guaycco que sube hasta el río que baja de Yaurisque y por dicha quebrada arriba sube hasta el cerro llamada *Viracocha-urcco* aguas vertientes del pueblo viejo de *Paccaric-tambo*" (A.M.A.C., exp. #17733:34v [1714]; my emphasis).

6. The following passages from the *composición de tierras* support the suggestion that the royal road was a boundary marker of *ayllu* lands:

in the *ayllu* of San Miguel in the place Urinca [there are] 2 *fanegadas* [a unit of land measure], in Accorque five *fanegadas* and in the place of Mayllaspay and Muchuchaqui 10 [*fanegadas*] that border on the *royal road that comes from the [territory] of Chumbivilcas.* (A.M.A.C., exp. #5877:13; my emphasis)

Item: 12 *fanegadas* that go from the boundary markers of the Indians of Naiva [Nayhua] all of which run from the old town of San Miguel and border with a low hill up to the said marker[s] and in another part [border] on the upper side with *the royal road from Cuzco* (A.M.A.C., exp. #5877:14; my emphasis)

7. The proceeding in question, dated 16 May 1659, concerns a dispute over a piece of land named Pallata. The owner of this property, Matheo Sanches de Medina, claimed that the land was in danger of being usurped by a neighboring hacienda owned by Angela del Castillo, the widow of Alonso Carrasco. In 1689, Pallata was identified as uncultivated *puna* land owned by three brothers, Tomás Sanches, Francisco Carrasco, and Pascual Sanches. In the document from 1689, Pallata was included within the territory of the ecclesiastical district (*doctrina*) of Yaurisque, rather than within the territory of Pacariqtambo, Yaurisque's one ecclesiastical annex (Villanueva Urteaga, 1982:465–467).

5. The Rituals and Ritual History of Divine Births and Boundaries

1. I thank Mr. Jean-Jacques Decoster, a graduate student in anthropology at Cornell University who served as my field assistant in 1987, for his descriptions of the preparation of the patron saint of the annex of P'irca (Santiago) on the occasion of this festival, and for his account of the actual journey of the saint to Pacariqtambo (an invigorating, early morning trot over some 10 kilometers of high and very rough terrain).

2. I should point out that Poole (1982:99–100) gives a highly restricted

representation of the "orbit of influence" of the festival of the Virgin of the Conception of Waynakancha, not even including within that territory the town of Pacariqtambo itself. Pacariqtambo does, in fact, send a dance troop to this festival every year. In addition, Decoster has noted (personal communication, 1987) that special drinking vessels used in this festival are brought from as far away as P'irca and Warubamba (along the Apurimac River, to the south of Pacariqtambo).

3. *K'eros* are wooden drinking vessels that are commonly used in Pacariqtambo to drink *chicha* on ritual occasions. *K'usilluqs* (of the monkey) are wooden drinking vessels carved in the shape of a monkey (or a monkey/man?) holding a cup on its head. These vessels are used in Pacariqtambo to consume *trago* (cane alcohol) only on important ritual occasions. I would like to thank Jean-Jacques Decoster, who provided the ethnographic notes on the festival of the Virgin of the Conception at the Hacienda Waynakancha on which this discussion is based.

4. The feast of the Virgin of the Purification—celebrated on February 2—commemorates the completion of the purification of the Virgin forty days after Christmas day (Cowie and Gummer, 1974:40, 157).

5. Sarmiento de Gamboa refers to this place by the name "Guanacancha" (1942[1572]:5); Cabello Valboa gives the toponym "Guamancancha" (1951 [1586]:261); and Murúa writes "Guaynac Cancha" (1962[1590]:21–24; cited in Urbano, 1981:94). In the documents collected for the census of ecclesiastical districts in the Cuzco area in 1689, we find references to lands in the *doctrina* of Yaurisque called "Uaynacancha," and to an hacienda called "Callancas" and "Uaynacancha" (Villanueva Urteaga, 1982:466). It seems clear from the contexts in which these toponyms appear (i.e., their associations with other place names) that they all refer to land(s) in the Yaurisque River Valley just to the north of Mollebamba and Ayllo Pachecti at or near the place known today as the Hacienda Waynakancha (cf. maps 2 and 3). Finally, it should be pointed out that in 1689, Waynakancha (as well as Mollebamba) was included within the territory of the *doctrina* of Yaurisque, not within that of the one annex of Yaurisque, Pacariqtambo (Villanueva Urteaga, 1982:465–471).

6. See Poole (1984:239–246) and Sallnow (1987:93–94, 131–132) for discussions of linkages between regional social organization and cycles of economic activities through ritual calendars in other communities in the circum-Cuzco region.

6. Conclusions

1. For similar interpretations of the "mythospatial" dimensions of the legendary journey of the ancestors from Pacariqtambo to Cuzco, see Zuidema (1986) and Urbano (1987). I should point out here that Urbano makes what I think is an unfounded and unwarranted assertion that the "Pacariqtambo" mentioned in the chronicles of Sarmiento de Gamboa, Cabello Valboa, Murúa et al. may be identified with the town of Ollantaytambo, which is

located in the Urubamba Valley to the north of Cuzco (Urbano, 1986, 1987). This suggestion clearly contradicts the testimony in Sarmiento and other post-Sarmiento chronicles and is directly refuted by the Inka noblemen in 1569 who testified on behalf of Rodrigo Sutiq Callapiña. This is not meant to suggest, however, that there were not *other* traditions of origin associated with Ollantaytambo (recall, for instance, the cycle of origin myths centering on Lake Titicaca).

Bibliography

Primary Sources

Archivo Arzobispado del Cuzco (A.A.C.)

1. "Informaciones contra Cura el Señor Dr. Don Pedro Crisologo de Villacorta," VIII.2.23, ff.78 (1772)
2. "Fábrica de la Iglesia de San Pedro de Paccarictambo, vice-parroquía de la doctrina de Yaurisque," 1836–1865 (s./n.); 50 fs.

Archivo Departamental del Cuzco, Cuzco (A.D.C.)

1. *Archivo del Ilustre Cabildo Justicia y Regimiento del Cuzco*, top. 8, sig. 3–5, años 1593–1597; fs.177
2. *Intendencia, Real Hacienda*, leg. ₋₀, 1792; s.n.
3. *Intendencia, Gobierno*, leg. 141, 1791–1792
   "La cuenta de tributos y Hospital del Partido de Chilques y Masques"
4. *Libros del Concejo Provincial del Cuzco*, no. 95, 1897
   "Contribución Predial Rústica, Provincia de Paruro"
5. *Tesorería Fiscal del Cuzco, Libros de Matrículos*, libros no. 1 y 2 (1831); libro no. 3 (1836), libro no. 4 (1850)
   "Extractos de Yndígenas, Provincia de Paruro"

Archivo del Ministerio de Agricultura, Cuzco (A.M.A.C.)

1. Expediente #2073, 1936
   "Expediente relativo a la queja organizada por los indígenas Carmen Llamacchima, Vicente Champi i otros, contra don Roman F. Baca . . ."
2. Expediente #4281, 1964
   "Expediente para el reconocimiento de la Comunidad de Ayllo-Pachecti o Mollebamba"
3. Expediente #5877, 1944
   "Expediente administrativo relativo al reconocimiento e inscripción oficial de la Comunidad de 'Paccarectambo,' del Distrito de Paruro, de la Provincia de Paruro, del Departamento del Cuzco"
4. Expediente #9288, 1946
   "La reclamación interpuesta por Don Mariano, Carmen Llamac-

chima, i otros de la comunidad de 'Paccaretambo,' contra Doña
Cabrilla Baca, Vda. de Baca, sobre despojo de tierras"
5. Expediente #17733, 1964
"Expediente relativo al reconocimiento e inscripción oficial de la
comunidad de indígenas de 'AYLLO-PACHECTI o MOLLEBAMBA'"

Archivo General de la Nación, Lima (A.G.N.)

Secondary Sources

Acosta, Antonio
    1987   "La extirpación de las idolatrías en el Perú. Origen y desarrollo de
            las campañas: A propósito de *Cultura andina y represión*, de
            Pierre Duviols." *Revista Andina* 9:171–195.
Adorno, Rolena
    1986   *Guaman Poma: Writing and Resistance in Colonial Peru.* Aus-
            tin: University of Texas Press.
Alberti Manzanares, Pilar
    1985   "La influencia económica y política de las Acllacuna en el Inca-
            nato." *Revista de Indias* 45, no. 176:557–585.
Allen, Catherine J.
    1984   "Patterned Time: The Mythic History of a Peruvian Commu-
            nity." *Journal of Latin American Lore* 10, no. 2:151–173.
    1988   *The Hold Life Has.* Washington, D.C.: Smithsonian Institution
            Press.
Ascher, Marcia, and Robert Ascher
    1975   "The Quipu as a Visible Language." *Visible Language* 9:329–356.
    1981   *Code of the Quipu.* Ann Arbor: University of Michigan Press.
Avila, Francisco de
    1966   *Dioses y hombres de Huarochirí* [1608]. Translated by J. M. Ar-
            guedas. Lima: Instituto de Estudios Peruanos.
Bauer, Brian S.
    1987   "Sistemas andinos de organización rural antes del estableci-
            miento de reducciones: El ejemplo de Pacariqtambo (Perú)." *Re-
            vista Andina* 9:197–210.
    n.d.   "Recent Archaeological Investigations in the Ruins of Mauka-
            llaqta, Department of Cusco." Manuscript.
Beattie, John
    1960   *Bunyoro, an African Kingdom.* New York: Holt, Rinehart &
            Winston.
Bertonio, Ludovico
    1984   *Vocabulario de la lengua aymara* [1612]. Cochabamba, Bolivia:
            Ediciones CERES.
Betanzos, Juan de
    1968   *Suma y narración de los Incas* [1551]. In *Crónicas peruanas de
            interés indígena.* Biblioteca de Autores Españoles, Vol. 209. Ma-
            drid: Ediciones Atlas.

Bingham, Hiram
  1930   *Machu Picchu: A Citadel of the Incas.* New Haven, Conn.: Yale
          University Press.
Cabello Valboa, Miguel
  1951   *Miscelánea antártica* [1586]. Lima: Universidad Nacional Mayor
          de San Marcos.
Callapiña, Supno, y otros Khipukamayuqs
  1974   *Relación de la descendencia, gobierno y conquista de los Incas*
          [1542/1608]. Prologue by Juan José Vega. Lima: Ediciones de la
          Biblioteca Universitaria.
Chardon, Roland
  1980   "The Elusive Spanish League: A Problem of Measurement in
          Sixteenth-Century New Spain." *Hispanic American Historical
          Review* 60, no. 2:294–302.
Cieza de León, Pedro de
  1967   *El señorío de los Incas* [1553]. Edited by C. Aranibar. Lima: In-
          stituto de Estudios Peruanos.
Cobo, Bernabé
  1964   *Historia del Nuevo Mundo* [1653]. Biblioteca de Autores Es-
          pañoles. Vol. 92. Madrid: Ediciones Atlas.
Cock C., Guillermo, and Mary E. Doyle
  1979   "Del culto solar a la clandestinidad de Inti e Punchao." *Historia y
          cultura* 12:51–73.
Cowie, L. W., and John S. Gummer
  1974   *The Christian Calendar.* Springfield, Mass.: G. & C. Merriam Co.
Cusihuamán, Antonio
  1976   *Diccionario Quechua Cuzco-Collao.* Lima: Instituto de Estudios
          Peruanos.
de Certeau, Michel
  1984   *The Practice of Everyday Life.* Berkeley & Los Angeles: Univer-
          sity of California Press.
de Heusch, Luc
  1982   *The Drunken King, or, the Origin of the State.* Bloomington: In-
          diana University Press.
Diez de San Miguel, Garci
  1964   *Visita hecha a la provincia de Chucuito* [1567]. Edited by John V.
          Murra. Lima: Casa de la Cultura del Perú.
Dumezil, Georges
  1977   *Gods of the Ancient Northmen* [1959]. Berkeley & Los Angeles:
          University of California Press.
Durán, Diego
  1964   *The Aztecs: The History of the Indies of New Spain.* Translated
          and edited by D. Heyden and F. Horcasitas. New York: Orion.
Duviols, Pierre
  1977   "Los nombres Quechua de Viracocha, supuesto 'Dios Creador' de
          los evangelizadores." *Allpanchis Phuturinqa* 10:53–64.
  1979a   "Datation, paternité et idéologie de la 'Declaración de los Quipu-

camayos a Vaca de Castro.'" In *Les cultures ibériques en devenir, essais publiès en homenage à la mémoire de Marcel Bataillon (1895–1977)*, pp. 583–591. Paris: La Fondation Singer-Polignac.

1979*b*   "La dinastía de los Incas: monarquía o diarquía? Argumentos heurísticos a favor de una tesis estructuralista." *Journal de la Société des Americanistes* 66.

1980   "La guerra entre el Cuzco y los Chanca: Historia o mito?" *Revista de la universidad Complutense* 28, no. 117:363–371.

Espinoza Soriano, Waldemar
1960   "El alcalde mayor indígena en el Virreinato del Perú." *Anuario de Estudios Americanos* 17:183–300.

Flores Galindo, Alberto
1986   *Europa y el país de los Incas: La utopía andina*. Lima: Instituto de Apoyo Agrario.

1987   "Comunidades y doctrínas: La disputa por las almas. Sierra Central (1608–1666)." In *Comunidades campesinas*, edited by H. Bonilla, et al., pp. 137–150. Chiclayo, Peru: Centro de Estudios Sociales Solidaridad.

Gade, Daniel W., and Mario Escobar
1982   "Village Settlement and the Colonial Legacy in Southern Peru." *Geographical Review* 72, no. 4:430–449.

Glave, Luis Miguel
1986   "Agricultura y capitalismo en la sierra sur del Perú (fines del siglo XIX y comienzos del XX)." In *Estados y naciones en los Andes*, edited by J. P. Deler and Y. Saint-Geours, vol. 1, pp. 213–244. Lima: Instituto de Estudios Peruanos.

1987   "Comunidades campesinas en el sur Andino, siglo XVII." In *Comunidades campesinas: Cambios y permanencias*, edited by H. Bonilla et al., pp. 61–94. Chiclayo, Peru: Centro de Estudios Sociales Solidaridad.

González Holguín, Diego
1952   *Vocabulario de la lengua general de todo el Perú llamada lengua Qquichua o del Inca* [1608]. Lima: Instituto de Historia, U.N.M.S.M.

Goody, Jack
1977   *The Domestication of the Savage Mind*. Cambridge: Cambridge University Press.

Guaman Poma de Ayala, Felipe
1980   *El primer nueva corónica y buen gobierno* [1583–1615]. Edited by J. V. Murra and R. Adorno. Mexico City: Siglo XXI.

Hampe Martínez, Teodoro
1986   "Sobre encomenderos y repartimientos en la diócesis de Lima a principios del siglo XVII." *Revista Andina* 7:173–194.

Hocart, A. M.
1970   *Kings and Councillors* [1936]. Chicago: University of Chicago Press.

Huertas Vallejos, Lorenzo
  1981   *La religión en una sociedad rural andina (siglo XVII)*. Ayacucho, Peru: Universidad Nacional San Cristóbal de Huamanga.
Hünefeldt, Christine
  1982   *Lucha por la tierra y protesta indígena: Las comunidades indígenas del Perú entre colonia y república*. Bonn: B.A.S.
Hyslop, John
  1979   "El área Lupaca bajo el dominio incaico: Un reconocimiento arqueológico." *Historica* 3, no. 1:53–78.
  1984   *The Inka Road System*. Orlando, Fla.: Academic Press.
Isbell, Billie Jean
  1977   " 'Those Who Love Me': An Analysis of Andean Kinship and Reciprocity within a Rural Context." In *Andean Kinship and Marriage*, edited by R. Bolton and E. Mayer, American Anthropological Association, Publication no. 7; pp. 81–105. Washington, D.C.: American Anthropological Association.
  1985   *To Defend Ourselves: Ecology and Ritual in an Andean Village* [1978]. Prospect Heights, Ill.: Waveland Press.
Iwasaki Cauti, Fernando
  1986   "Las panacas del Cuzco y la pintura incaica." *Revista de Indias* 46, no. 177:59–74.
Jiménez de la Espada, Marcos
  1892   *Una antigüalla peruana*. Madrid: Tipografía de Manuel Ginés Hernández.
Julien, Catherine J.
  1982   "Inca Decimal Administration in the Lake Titicaca Region." In *The Inca and Aztec States, 1400–1800*, edited by G. A. Collier, R. I. Rosaldo, and J. D. Wirth, pp. 119–151. New York: Academic Press.
Kater, Marijke
  n.d.   "Informe preliminar del estudio económico-social del cultivo de la papa en la comunidad de Paccarectambo en la provincia de Paruro: La desaparición de la papa huayco." Manuscript.
  1988   "De Ongelijke Strijd Tussen Twee Landbouwsystemen." M.A. thesis, University of Amsterdam.
MacCormack, Sabine
  1984   "From the Sun of the Incas to the Virgin of Copacabana." *Representations* 8:30–60.
  1985   " 'The Heart Has Its Reasons': Predicaments of Missionary Christianity in Early Colonial Peru." *Hispanic American Historical Review* 65, no. 3:443–466.
Málaga Medina, Alejandro
  1979   "Aspecto urbano de las reducciones toledanas." *Revista de Historia de América* 88:167–183.
Mallon, Florencia
  1983   *The Defense of Community in Peru's Central Highlands*. Peas-

    ant Struggle and Capitalist Transition, 1860–1940. Princeton,
    N.J.: Princeton University Press.
Mesa, José de, and Teresa Gisbert
    1982   *Historia de la pintura cuzqueña.* Vol. I. Lima: Fundación Au-
            gusto N. Wiese, Banco Wiese Ltdo.
Meyerson, Julia L.
    1990   *'Tambo: Life in an Andean Village.* Austin: University of Texas
            Press.
Molina, Cristóbal de
    1943   *Fábulas y ritos de los Incas* [1575]. Los Pequeños Grandes Li-
            bros de Historia Americana, 1st series, vol. IV. Lima: Imprenta
            Miranda.
Muelle, Jorge C.
    1950   "Pacarectambo, apuntes de viaje." *Revista del Museo Nacional,
            Lima* 14:153–160.
Murra, John V.
    1975   "Un reino aymara en 1567." In *Formaciones económicas y po-
            líticas del mundo andino,* edited by J. V. Murra, pp. 193–223.
            Lima: Instituto de Estudios Peruanos.
Murúa, Martín
    1946   *Los orígenes de los Inkas* [1590]. Los Pequeños Grandes Libros de
            Historia Americana, 1st series, Vol. II. Lima: Imprenta Miranda.
    1962   *Historia general del Perú, origen y descendencia de los Incas*
            [1590]. Vol. I, Biblioteca Americana Vetus. Madrid: Instituto Gon-
            zalo Fernández de Oviedo.
Navarro del Aguila, Víctor
    1983   *Las tribus de Ankcu Wallokc* [1939]. Lima: Ediciones Atusparía.
Niles, Susan A.
    1987   *Callachaca: Style and Status in an Inca Community.* Iowa City:
            University of Iowa Press.
Ohnuki-Tierney, Emiko
    1987   *The Monkey as Mirror: Symbolic Transformations in Japanese
            History and Ritual.* Princeton, N.J.: Princeton University Press.
Oricaín, Pablo José
    1906   "Compendio breve de discursos varios sobre diferentes mate-
            rias y noticias geográficas comprehensivas á este obispado del
            Cuzco . . ." [1790]. In *Juicio de límites entre el Perú y Bolivia.* 11.
            Obispados y Audencia del Cuzco, edited by Víctor M. Maurtua,
            pp. 319–377. Barcelona: Imprenta de Henrich y Comp.
Pachacuti Yamqui Salcamaygua, Joan de Santa Cruz
    1950   *Relación de antigüedades deste reyno del Perú* [1613]. Biblioteca
            de Autores Españoles, no. 209. Madrid: Ediciones Atlas.
Pardo, Luis A.
    1946   "La metropoli de Paccarictambu: el adoratorio de Tamputtocco
            y el itinerario del camino seguido por los hermanos Ayar." *Re-
            vista de la Sección Arqueológica de la Universidad Nacional del
            Cuzco,* no. 2:3–46.

1957   *Historia y arqueología del Cuzco.* Two volumes. Cuzco: Imprenta Colegio Militar Leonicio Prado.

Pease, Franklin

1973   *El dios creador andino.* Lima: Mosca Azul Editores.

1977   *Collaguas I.* Edited by F. Pease. Lima: Pontificia Universidad Católica del Perú.

Polo de Ondegardo, Juan

1916   *Relación de los fundamentos acerca del notable daño. . . . Informaciones acerca de la religión y gobierno de los Incas* [1571]. Colección de Libros y Documentos Referentes a la Historia del Perú. Series I, vol. 3; pp. 49–55. Lima: Imprenta y Librería Sanmartí.

Poole, Deborah A.

1982   "Los santuarios religiosos en la economía regional andina." *Allpanchis Phuturinqa* 19:75–116.

1984   "Ritual-Economic Calendars in Paruro: The Structure of Representation in Andean Ethnography." Ph.D. dissertation, University of Illinois, Urbana-Champaign.

1987   "Korilazos, abigeos y comunidades campesinas en la Provincia de Chumbivilcas (Cusco)." In *Comunidades campesinas,* edited by H. Bonilla et al., pp. 257–295. Chiclayo, Peru: Centro de Estudios Sociales Solidaridad.

Porras Barrenechea, Raúl

1986   *Los cronistas del Perú (1528–1650).* Biblioteca Clasicos del Perú, no. 2. Lima: Banco de Crédito del Perú.

Ramírez, Susan E.

1987   "The *'Dueño de Indios':* Thoughts on the Consequences of the Shifting Bases of Power of the *'Curaca de los Viejos Antiguos'* under the Spanish in Sixteenth-Century Peru." *Hispanic American Historical Review* 67, no. 4:575–610.

Ramos Gavilán, Fray Alonso

1976   *Historia de Nuestra Señora de Copacabana* [1621]. La Paz: Academia Boliviana de la Historia.

Randall, Robert

1987   "Del tiempo y del río: el ciclo de la historia y la energía en la cosmología incaica." *Boletín de Lima,* no. 54:69–95.

n.d.   "The Mythstory of Kuri Qoyllur: Sex, Seqes and Sacrifice in Inka Agricultural Festivals." Manuscript.

Rosaldo, Renato

1980   *Ilongot Headhunting, 1883–1974.* Stanford, Cal.: Stanford University Press.

Rostworowski de Diez Canseco, María

1981   "La voz parcialidad en su contexto en los siglos XVI y XVII." In *Etnohistoria y antropología andina,* edited by Amalia Castelli, pp. 35–45. Lima: Centro de Proyección Cristiana.

1983   *Estructuras andinas del poder.* Lima: Instituto de Estudios Peruanos.

Rowe, John H.
1945   "Absolute Chronology in the Andean Area." *American Antiquity* 10, no. 3 : 265–284.
1946   "Inca Culture at the Time of the Spanish Conquest." In *Handbook of South American Indians.* B.A.E., Bulletin 143, vol. II : 183–330. Washington, D.C.
1957   "The Incas under Spanish Colonial Institutions." *Hispanic American Historical Review* 37, no. 2 : 155–199.
1980   "An account of the Shrines of Ancient Cuzco." *Ñawpa Pacha* 17 : 1–80.
1981   "Una relación de los adoratorios del antiguo Cuzco." *Histórica* 5, no. 2 : 209–261 (Spanish version of Rowe, 1980).
1985a   "La constitución inca del Cuzco." *Histórica* 9, no. 1 : 35–74.
1985b   "Probanza de los Incas nietos de conquistadores." *Histórica* 9, no. 2 : 193–245.
Sahlins, Marshall
1981   *Historical Metaphors and Mythical Realities.* Ann Arbor: University of Michigan Press.
1985   *Islands of History.* Chicago: University of Chicago Press.
Saignes, Thierry
1987   "De la borrachera al retrato: Los caciques andinos entre dos legitimidades (Charcas)." *Revista Andina* 9 : 139–170.
Sallnow, Michael J.
1987   *Pilgrims of the Andes: Regional Cults in Cusco.* Washington, D.C.: Smithsonian Institution Press.
Salomon, Frank
1985   "Idolaters and Rebels: A Problem in Andean Culture and Politics." Paper prepared for the Workshop on the Political Economy of Latin America, Center for Industrial Societies, University of Chicago, January.
Sarmiento de Gamboa, Pedro
1942   *Historia de los Incas* [1572]. Buenos Aires: Emecé Editores.
Schaedel, Richard P.
1978   "Formation of the Inca State." In *El Hombre y la Cultura Andina,* edited by Ramiro Matos M., vol. I, pp. 112–156.
Silverblatt, Irene M.
1981   "Moon, Sun, and Devil: Inca and Colonial Transformations of Andean Gender Relations." Ph.D. dissertation, University of Michigan, Ann Arbor.
Sistema Nacional de Apoyo a la Movimiento Social Lima.
1976   *Directorio de comunidades campesinas.*
Skar, Harald
1982   *The Warm Valley People: Duality and Land Reform among the Quechua Indians of Highland Peru.* New York: Columbia University Press.

Soukup, Jaroslav
 1970   *Vocabulario de los nombres vulgares de la flora peruana.* Lima: Colegio Salesiano.
Spalding, Karen
 1984   *Huarochirí: An Andean Society under Inca and Spanish Rule.* Stanford, Cal.: Stanford University Press.
Stern, Steve J.
 1982*a*   *Peru's Indian Peoples and the Challenge of Spanish Conquest.* Madison: University of Wisconsin Press.
 1982*b*   "The Social Significance of Judicial Institutions in an Exploitative Society: Huamanga, Peru, 1570–1640." In *The Inca and Aztec States, 1400–1800,* edited by G. Collier and R. Wirth, pp. 289–320. San Francisco: Academic Press.
Toledo, Francisco de
 1867   *Relaciones de los vireyes y audiencias que han gobernado el Perú. I. Memorial y ordenanzas de D. Francisco de Toledo* [1573]. Lima: Imprenta del Estado por J. E. del Campo.
 1920   *Informaciones sobre el antiguo Perú* [1572–1575]. Libros y Documentos Referentes a la Historia del Perú, 2d series, vol. III. Lima: Librería e Imprenta Gil.
 1975   *Tasa de la visita general* [1583]. Introduction and paleography by Noble David Cook. Lima: Universidad Nacional Mayor de San Marcos.
Ulloa, Luis
 1909   "Documentos del Virrey Toledo: Visita general de los yndios del Cuzco, año del 1571, provincia Condesuyo." *Revista Histórica* 2:332–347.
Urbano, Henrique
 1981   *Wiracocha y Ayar: Héroes y funciones en las sociedades andinas.* Cuzco: Centro "Bartolomé de las Casas."
 1986   "La invención andina del hombre, de la cultura y de la sociedad y los ciclos miticos judeocristianos." *Boletín de Lima* 46:51–60.
 1987   "Qollana, Payan y Cayao. Lógica y sociedad en los Andes." *Boletín de Lima* 51:18–26.
 1988   "Thunupa, Taguapaca, Cachi: Introducción a un espacio simbólico andino." *Revista Andina* 11:201–224.
Urton, Gary
 1978   "Orientation in Quechua and Incaic Astronomy." *Ethnology* 17, no. 2:157–167.
 1981   *At the Crossroads of the Earth and the Sky: An Andean Cosmology.* Latin American Monographs series, no. 55. Austin: University of Texas Press.
 1984   "*Chuta:* El espacio de la práctica social en Pacariqtambo, Perú." *Revista Andina* 2, no. 1:7–56.
 1985*a*   "Animal Metaphors and the Life Cycle in an Andean Community." In *Animal Myths and Metaphors in South America,* edited

by Gary Urton, pp. 251–284. Salt Lake City: University of Utah Press.

1985b   "Festival Calendars and the Ritual Construction of Hierarchy in Pacariqtambo, Peru." Paper presented at the meetings of the American Society for Ethnohistory, Chicago.

1986   "Calendrical Cycles and Their Projections in Pacariqtambo, Peru." *Journal of Latin American Lore* 12, no. 1 : 45–64.

1988   "La arquitectura pública como texto social: La historia de un muro de adobe en Pacariqtambo, Perú (1915–1985)." *Revista Andina* 6, no. 1 : 225–263.

n.d.a   "Communal Cash-Cropping and Social Cohesion in Pacariqtambo." Manuscript.

n.d.b   "The Stranger in Andean Communities." In *Hommage au Professeur Pierre Duviols*, edited by R. Thiercelin, in press.

Vaca de Castro, Cristóbal

1929   *Discurso sobre la descendencia y gobierno de los Incas* [1542/ 1608]. Colección de Libros y Documentos Referentes a la Historia del Perú, 2d series, vol. III. Lima: Imprenta y Librería Sanmartí.

Valera, Blas

1950   *Relación de las costumbres antiguas de los naturales del Pirú* [ca. 1590]. In *Tres relaciones de Antigüedades peruanas*, edited by Marcos Jiménez de la Espada, pp. 135–203. Asunción, Paraguay: Editorial Guaranía.

Vansina, Jan

1965   *Les anciens royaumes de la savane*. Kinshasa, Zaire: Université Lovanium, Institut de Recherches Économiques et Sociales.

Villanueva Urteaga, Horacio

1982   *Cuzco, 1689. Economía y sociedad en el sur andino.* Cuzco: Centro de Estudios Rurales Andinos, "Bartolomé de las Casas."

Villarán, Manuel Vicente

1964   *Apuntes sobre la realidad social de los indígenas del Perú ante las leyes de Indias.* Lima: Talleres Gráficos P. L. Villanueva.

Wachtel, Nathan

1971   *La visión des Vaincus.* Paris: Editions Gallimard.

1986   "Men of the Water: The Uru Problem (Sixteenth and Seventeenth Centuries)." In *Anthropological History of Andean Polities*, edited by J. V. Murra, N. Wachtel, J. Revel, pp. 283–310. Cambridge: Cambridge University Press.

Watson, William

1964   *Tribal Cohesion in a Money Economy.* New York: Humanities Press.

Wedin, Åke

1963   *La cronología de la historia incaica.* Madrid: Instituto Ibero-Americano Gotemburgo Suecia.

Zamora, Margarita

1988   *Language, Authority and Indigenous History in the Comentarios Reales de los Incas.* Cambridge: Cambridge University Press.

Zuidema, R. T.
1964   *The Ceque System of Cuzco.* Leiden: E. J. Brill.
1973   "The Origin of the Inca Empire." In *Les grands empires;* Recueils de la Société Jean Bodin pour L'Histoire Comparative des Institutions, vol. XXXI:733–757. Brussels: Ed. Libraire Encyclopédique.
1977   "The Inca Kinship System: A New Theoretical View." In *Andean Kinship and Marriage,* edited by R. Bolton and E. Mayer, pp. 240–281. Washington, D.C.: American Anthropological Association, pub. no. 7.
1982a   "Bureaucracy and Systematic Knowledge in Andean Civilization." In *The Inca and Aztec States, 1400–1800,* edited by G. A. Collier, R. I. Rosaldo, J. D. Wirth, pp. 419–458. New York: Academic Press.
1982b   "Catachillay: The Role of the Pleiades and of the Southern Cross and α and β Centauri in the Calendar of the Incas." In *Ethnoastronomy and Archaeoastronomy in the American Tropics,* edited by A. Aveni and G. Urton. Annals of the New York Academy of Sciences, vol. 385:203–230. New York.
1982c   "Myth and History in Ancient Peru." In *The Logic of Culture,* edited by I. Rossi, pp. 150–175. South Hadley, Mass.: Bergin and Garvey Publishers.
1983   "Hierarchy and Space in Incaic Social Organization." *Ethnohistory* 30, no. 2:49–75.
1986   *La civilisation inca au Cuzco.* Essais et Conférences, Collège de France. Paris: Presses Universitaires de France.
n.d.   "The Moiety System of Inca Cuzco." Manuscript.
Zuidema, R. T., and Deborah A. Poole
1982   "Los límites de los cuatro suyus incaicos en el Cusco." *Bulletin de Institute Français des Etudes Andines* 11, nos. 1–2:83–89.
Zuidema, R. T., and Gary Urton
1976   "La constelación de la llama en los Andes peruanos." *Allpanchis Phuturinqa* 9:59–119.

Index

descendants of, 66–68; historicity of, 7, 9, 62; and Qori Kukas, 54, 55, 60–61, 62
pachamama, 60
Pachecti, 33, 35, 86; archaeological site, 85; *ayllu* of Pacariqtambo, 72, 80, 83, 86, 88, 94, 146; stopping place of Inka ancestors, 31, 37, 52, 87, 88, 105, 116, 120. *See also* Ayllo Pachecti; Mollebamba-Ayllo Pachecti
Pallata, 29, 38, 82, 87, 92, 93, 94, 97, 101, 105, 120, 147
Palomino, Luis, 89
panaqa, 20, 57, 60, 65, 67, 68, 123, 142
paqarikuy, 98
paqarina, 19, 31
Pardo, L. A., 33, 34, 114, 143
Paruro, 28, 42, 76, 90, 103, 146
Pascac, Domingo, 64–68, 127, 133, 145
patron saints, 87, 98, 101, 105, 108. *See also* saints
Paullu Inka, 45
payan, 57
Pease, F., 75, 141
pilgrimages, 96, 97, 98, 105, 108, 113, 114, 116, 117. *See also* ritual circuits
P'irca: annex, 103; *ayllu*, 72, 82, 83, 103, 147, 148
Pizarro Yupanque, Juan, 64, 65, 68, 134, 136, 145
planting, 59, 101, 106, 107, 108, 111, 114, 118
Polo de Ondegardo, J., 20
Poole, D. A., 24, 27, 28, 42, 58, 73, 89, 99, 100, 103, 104, 143, 145, 147, 148
Porras Barrenechea, R., 32, 43, 44, 45, 143
positional succession, 7, 8
pre-Inka, 26, 27, 85
provincial, 13, 14, 15, 28, 67, 105
puma, 33

Pumatambo, 72, 79, 81, 82, 83, 85, 86, 108, 112
Pumaurqu, 32–37, 52, 89, 94, 120, 128, 143
pururawka, 54, 57, 59
pururuna, 54

qachun, 23
Qarhuacalla (annex and *ayllu*), 72, 80, 83, 85, 90, 112, 146; *ayllu* affiliation of Inkas-by-Privilege, 50, 52, 88, 105, 129, 130, 131, 134, 135, 137, 139; ranking of, 72, 80. *See also* Qarhuacalla Primero; Qarhuacalla Segundo
Qarhuacalla Primero, 72, 80, 104, 107
Qarhuacalla Segundo, 72, 79, 80, 81, 85, 86, 107, 108, 112
qatay, 23, 81
Qhapaq T'oqo, 20
Qoipa, 72, 76, 82, 83, 85–86
qollana, 57, 79
Qollasuyu, 57, 121
Qolqueuqru, 82
Qorikancha, 57, 58, 121
Qori Kuka, 47, 49, 50, 54–61, 62, 68. *See also* Chañan Qori Kuka; Qoya Qori Kuka
Qori Qoyllur, 47, 53, 129, 130, 132, 134, 135, 138, 139
qoya, 47, 49
Qoya Qori Kuka, 60, 61, 62, 68, 123, 130, 132, 133, 137
Quechua, 19, 22, 141
Quinhuara (*ayllu*), 72, 83, 92, 93, 104, 108
Quirirmanta, 38, 120
Quisco, 143

rainbow, 38
Ramírez, S. E., 125
Ramos Gavilán, F. A., 38, 45
Randall, R., 53, 98, 142, 145
reducción (reduction), 32, 41, 75; *ayllus* included within, of